Ferdinand Hodler

Peter Lorenz s.j.

Published by University Art Museum, Berkeley, 1972.
All rights reserved. Library of Congress card
catalogue number 72–619599.

Peter Selz
University Art Museum, Berkeley

with contributions by
Jura Brüschweiler
Phyllis Hattis
Eva Wyler

Ferdinand Hodler

(overleaf) Ferdinand Hodler painting a study for
"Unanimity" (ca. 1912). [Photo by Moos Frères,
Geneva. © Jura Brüschweiler, Geneva].

This monograph on Ferdinand Hodler is dedicated to the memory of Alberto Giacometti.

Schedule of the Exhibition

University Art Museum, Berkeley
November 22, 1972 – January 7, 1973

The Solomon R. Guggenheim Museum,
New York
February 2 – April 8, 1973

Busch-Reisinger Museum, Harvard
University, Cambridge
May 1 – June 22, 1973

Special Credits

Eva Wyler, Associate for the Ferdinand
Hodler Exhibition

A Selection Committee was formed to
assist with the determination of Hodler
works to be exhibited. The Committee
consisted of Jura Brüschweiler, Phyllis
Hattis, Peter Selz (Chairman), and
Eva Wyler.

The exhibition was sponsored by and
organized with the active cooperation of
Pro Helvetia Foundation in Zurich, an
institution created by the Swiss Confederation, whose first task is the promotion
of cultural relations with foreign
countries. Financial support for the
project was provided by Pro Helvetia
Foundation in Zurich, and by numerous
Swiss and American public and private
institutions and individuals.

This project was also supported by a grant
from the National Endowment for the
Arts in Washington, D.C., a Federal
agency.

Table of Contents

9 Acknowledgments
by Peter Selz

11 Prefatory Note
by Thomas M. Messer, Daniel Robbins, and Peter Selz

13 Introduction: A Look at Ferdinand Hodler
by Eva Wyler

15 Ferdinand Hodler: Painter
by Peter Selz

71 Ferdinand Hodler: Draftsman
by Phyllis Hattis

107 Ferdinand Hodler: Writer
Introducing a Few Texts by the Artist
by Jura Brüschweiler

111 A Selection from the Writings of Ferdinand Hodler
compiled and edited by Jura Brüschweiler

111 The Painter's Decalogue (1874–1875)
111 Physiognomy of Landscape (1885–1886?)
113 Barthélemy Menn/Beginnings/
Artistic Temperament (1891)
115 My Present Tendencies/Night (1891)
117 Interview: Ferdinand Hodler on his
Principles of Art and on Klimt (1904)
118 Last Notes (1917–1918)
119 The Mission of the Artist (1897)

127 Chronology
by Jura Brüschweiler

129 Selected Bibliography
by Jura Brüschweiler

131 Catalogue to the Exhibition

140 Lenders and Contributors to the Exhibition

Acknowledgments

Peter Selz
Director, University Art Museum, Berkeley,
November 1972

In 1969 when I first became aware of the large and monumental spaces of the new University Art Museum, I realized with great satisfaction that one of my long-standing ambitions—the introduction of the work of Ferdinand Hodler to the American public—could be achieved in an environment eminently suitable to the heroic paintings of this modern master. At the same time Eva Wyler in New York began formulating plans for a Hodler exhibition, and we decided to make common cause and pool our ideas toward the realization of this major project. Ms. Wyler, who became Associate for the Ferdinand Hodler Exhibition, proceeded to make initial contacts with the relevant museums and private collectors in Switzerland, whom I want to thank for their extraordinary generosity in parting with their possessions for a period of time sufficiently extended to make it possible to show Hodler's work in three important American museums. The names of the lenders appear on page 140.

Eva Wyler also worked with tireless devotion in raising the necessary funds from public and private sources in Switzerland to make this project a reality (a complete list of the contributors appears on page 140). Ms. Wyler, who has been involved for over two years on virtually a full-time basis, has contributed so significantly and in so many ways that it is impossible to itemize her efforts. She has given freely of her time and energy to coordinate all phases of the exhibition, and her assistance and cooperation have been essential to the culmination of the Hodler project.

A project such as this also needed a great deal of scholarly advice. Above all, I want to express my gratitude to Mr. Jura Brüschweiler of Geneva for his constant help throughout the undertaking. Mr. Brüschweiler, who had also long hoped for an exhibition to introduce Hodler's work to America, greeted our plans with the most generous cooperation and enthusiasm. All titles and dates were established by him, he wrote a new essay for this catalogue, prepared the chronology and bibliography, and, as the expert scholar performing the liaison function with the essential sources in Switzerland, contributed significantly to making possible the loan of 67 paintings and 51 drawings. Mr. Brüschweiler, who has devoted a great many years to research on Hodler's work, generously made available his complete personal Hodler archives, and supplied previously unpublished photographs, documentation, and manuscripts by the artist, as well as the original version of the renowned Fribourg lecture.

The exhibition could not have been realized without the effective help from the Pro Helvetia Foundation, Zurich, acting through its director, Mr. Luc Boissonnas. Mr. Boissonnas contributed significantly through unstinting personal effort to making this exhibition a memorable cultural link between our countries, involving as it does some of Switzerland's national treasure.

I wish to acknowledge the valuable help received from

Dr. Phyllis Hattis, who not only made the selection of the
drawings for the show and wrote the perceptive analysis of
the drawings in the monograph, but who, together with Jura
Brüschweiler and Eva Wyler, also assisted me in making
the selection of paintings.

Among our friends in Switzerland, I am especially grateful to
the directors of Switzerland's four major museums in Basel,
Bern, Geneva, and Zurich, as well as to the Gottfried Keller
Foundation, which owns many of Hodler's best paintings.
Mr. Josef Müller of Solothurn, who owns one of the finest
collections of Hodler paintings, is another person who must be
singled out for his aid and encouragement. To Dr. Hans Lüthy
and his staff at the Schweizerisches Institut für Kunstwissen-
schaft in Zurich are due my thanks for their indispensable
help and assistance.

The consular representatives of Switzerland in the home cities
of the museums that will show the Hodler exhibition have been
most helpful: Mr. Jean Studer, Consul General of Switzerland
in San Francisco, where the show is originating; His Excellency,
Ambassador Pierre-Henri Aubaret, Consul General of Switzerland in New York; and Dr. Freddy Homburger, Consul of
Switzerland in Boston.

I have many more people to thank for their aid in preparing
this exhibition and monograph. Brenda Richardson, Assistant
Director/Curatorial of this Museum staff coordinated the
planning and progress of the exhibition and publication. Joy
Feinberg, Registrar of this Museum, was responsible for over-
seeing the movement and safekeeping of the paintings from
Europe throughout the United States and back to their home
base. Madeline Jay did most of the translations of Hodler's and
Jura Brüschweiler's texts into English. Agnes Mongan, Director
Emeritus of the Fogg Art Museum, generously gave of her time
and judgment in her critical reading of the essay on Hodler's
draftsmanship. Lorna Price edited the manuscripts, and Bruce
Montgomery designed the catalogue. Hildegarde Fuss, Enid
Larson, Jane Nicholson, Barbara Dorsey, Marilyn Kaye Hodson,
Dale Munday, Catherine Fuller, Fred Altshuler, Roderick Hall,
Elizabeth Rosenwald, Dr. Joseph R. Goldyne, and Maya Bar-
Hillel were most helpful in aiding us in dealing with the many
details pertinent to the preparation of the exhibition and
catalogue.

Thomas M. Messer, Director of The Solomon R. Guggenheim
Museum in New York, and Daniel Robbins, Director of the
Fogg and Busch-Reisinger Museums at Harvard University,
were most supportive in their participation in this project.
All these people must be given credit for launching this exhibition and making it possible for the paintings of this great Swiss
artist to be brought to the attention of a wider public so that
his work can be studied, re-experienced, and enjoyed.

Prefatory Note

Thomas M. Messer
Director, The Solomon R. Guggenheim
Museum, New York

Daniel Robbins
Director, Busch-Reisinger Museum and
Fogg Art Museum, Harvard University,
Cambridge, Massachusetts

Peter Selz
Director, University Art Museum,
University of California, Berkeley

Why should a relatively unknown Swiss painter, born some 120 years ago, now be exhibited in three major American museums from coast to coast? Is our understanding of the development of modern painting, particularly at the turn of the century, going to be broadened substantially through exhibiting a comprehensive retrospective of the paintings and drawings of Ferdinand Hodler (1853–1918)?

Many of the artists born during the middle of the past century turned from the representation of tangible reality toward the evocative suggestion of feeling and the concern with Idea, Thought, Style, Morality. The Symbolist generation—poets like Mallarmé and Rimbaud, composers like Debussy, Mahler, and Satie, painters like Gauguin, Munch, and Hodler—were committed to spiritual content. Their art often deals with the meaning of life and the presence of death. Above all, the Symbolists in all fields of expression shared a desire to create a new formal language in which to clothe their cosmic aspirations, their pantheist thoughts. They developed a style, sometimes elusive, sometimes very definite, which would reach what Gauguin called the "mysterious center of thought."

Hodler's large and ambitious choreographic murals, his incisive portraits of the living and the dead, his renditions of mountains where a robust realism is used to express the mystique of the Alpine landscape, are a significant part of a period which is now being re-evaluated. Symbolism commands so much of our attention today, perhaps because our own period is engaged in a new search for non-materialist, even mystic values.

Ferdinand Hodler has long been recognized in Central Europe as a major figure in the Symbolist movement. Almost his entire output is in public and private collections in Switzerland. His style and message seemed heavy and often didactic to generations whose sensibilities were trained by the painting of France. For these reasons among others the art of Hodler has remained relatively unknown in the United States.

We salute our Swiss colleagues and all of those who contributed toward the realization of this project. The opportunity of introducing this major artist to an American audience is indeed a welcome occasion.

63. *Self-portrait.* (1917). Oil on board mounted
    on canvas. 15¼ x 12⅜″. Musée d'Art et
    d'Histoire, Geneva.

Introduction:
A Look at
Ferdinand Hodler

Eva Wyler
Associate for the Ferdinand Hodler Exhibition

Switzerland's rich cultural tradition produced few great artists. Of these, most developed abroad and there gained fame: Holbein and Füssli (Fuseli) in England; Giacometti and Le Corbusier in France; Böcklin and Klee in Germany. Ferdinand Hodler is the exception. He stayed: he painted the mountains and lakes, the history and the people of his homeland, and instilled vitality into this traditional subject matter. Indeed, Hodler broke away completely from the provincialism of Swiss painting of the preceding decades. He created a forceful and original idiom which influenced the generation of Swiss painters that followed him. With Puvis de Chavannes, he was the most important innovator of modern monumental painting. He was an exponent of Jugendstil, and he was recognized as a precursor of Expressionism. The Swiss see in Hodler their first great modern painter; to them his work, in its forthrightness of expression and its imagery, mirrors the essential quality of their nation.

This man, roughhewn, self-taught, aspiring, born of Switzerland's proletariat, who began his career as a painter of views for tourists, created a painting of bold images and a sense of tremendous energy. A marked idealism combines with an essentially realistic mode of representation, a plastic feeling of form with a linear treatment of surface. Hodler's idealism, expressed as a conviction of man's common destiny, of his equality before the great forces of nature, and of the underlying unity of all things, was in direct response to the harshness of his life and to the specter of tragedy that overshadowed it—an idealism nourished also by philosophical ideas that had currency among fin-de-siècle artists and thinkers. That attitude is apparent in his earliest works as a sense of heightened significance that attaches itself to the subject depicted. Hodler did not achieve this affect through emotional intensity but, on the contrary, through a detached and highly ordered treatment of the subject matter, which imbued it with an almost magical sense of power. Later, his concern with transcendent values was manifested by frankly symbolical and allegorical compositions, but in a manner that remains cool and almost cerebral.

This coolness and objectivity of language conform perfectly with his temperament and outlook. Hodler was faced early in life with stern realities, but also he was endowed with the strength to cope with them. Hence, he was not a romantic, not given to introspection or to great subtleties of feeling. He sought the concrete, the tactile: painting for him was a means of asserting himself, of dominating his world. With the monumental scale Hodler found his best expression. It answered his need to be objective and impersonal; it lent itself to a painting of ideas; and it accommodated the energy and assertiveness of his temperament. The public responded: his first large-scale symbolic painting, *Night* of 1890, drew attention in Paris; his recognition in Switzerland and subsequently abroad in Germany and Austria was spread further with *The Retreat from Marignano*, the fresco he created for the Schweizerisches Landesmuseum in Zurich. His European reputation as a master of modern art was founded on his monumental and symbolical works.

Ferdinand Hodler was not in the mainstream of European art. He was isolated from it. Not within, but alongside the mainstream, Hodler's art became significant because of what he achieved through his talent and the force of his vision.

Hodler exhibited widely in Europe during his lifetime, and from about 1900 enjoyed a European reputation, with a devoted following especially in Germany and Austria. After 1914 his fame declined abroad. In Switzerland he continued to be honored as the country's greatest painter and was viewed as an artist of international stature for many years after his death. Eventually, however, the revolutionary discoveries of twentieth-century art shifted this perspective even in his homeland.

Hodler is relatively unknown in America. Recent major exhibitions of his work in Switzerland, Vienna, and London suggest a renewed interest in this artist that will lead to a re-evaluation of his work. Our knowledge of the development of modern art is incomplete without a recognition of his contribution, which the present exhibition—the first retrospective museum exhibition on this continent—intends to illuminate.

Ferdinand Hodler: Painter

Peter Selz

In 1913, just before the outbreak of World War I, President Poincaré of France personally decorated Ferdinand Hodler with the "Légion d'Honneur" when he exhibited at the Salon d'Automne in Paris. During the same year the German Kaiser was present for the unveiling of the Swiss painter's large mural in Hannover. Hodler had met Rodin and Degas; he was celebrated in Vienna when he was the featured artist of the Vienna Secession exhibition in 1904. He was acclaimed by Gustav Klimt and exerted a certain influence on Egon Schiele. Emil Nolde, Alexej von Jawlensky, and the German Expressionists in general acknowledged their debt to the Swiss master. Indeed, he was compared to Cézanne as one of the giants of early twentieth-century art. More recently, Alberto Giacometti paid homage to his great Swiss predecessor.

Hodler is unique among the artists of the late nineteenth century. He came from a very isolated place, he was never part of any artistic community, had little tradition to continue or even to rebel against. He was not only a self-taught artist, but also a self-generated individual, who would follow his own vision of his mission and managed, quite fortuitously, to meet individuals who willingly would help him. Coming from the city of Bern, uneducated and poverty-stricken, he must have possessed potent inner resources and energies he could tap to overcome the inertia of the circumstances of his birth and upbringing.

Ferdinand Hodler was born into the Swiss proletariat in the poorest quarter of Bern in 1853. His father, an impecunious carpenter, died when the artist was still a child, and was eventually followed in death by his mother, who was remarried to Gottlieb Schüpbach, a widowed house and sign painter. Of the twelve children in these combined households, Ferdinand and five others survived; the rest died in infancy and youth, most of them of tuberculosis. The image of death was ingrained in Hodler's mind and vision: he was to paint it in many versions throughout his life.

From his eighth year, Ferdinand helped Schüpbach in his work. At about the age of fifteen, in 1868, he was apprenticed to Ferdinand Sommer, a painter of mountain views—perhaps not as unusual a transition from the stepfather's paint shop as it might seem at first glance: paintings of landscape for sale to tourists were the precursors of the landscape photographs of today. During the three years of Hodler's apprenticeship, Sommer conveyed to the young artist the rudiments of painting. But Hodler, despite the deprivation of his childhood, was eager to learn about art, science, religion, and life. Hoping to leave humdrum provincial existence behind him, he decided in 1872 to leave the Swiss countryside near Bern. He walked to Geneva without money, without education, with the slightest knowledge of French, and without a friend to greet him at his destination. He knew only that Geneva was a cultural center of considerable importance and that it might be a place where, having left behind the sadness of his childhood, he could hope to enter a new life, perhaps as a new person. (It is interesting to note that Gottlieb Schüpbach had left Switzerland in 1871 after the death of Hodler's mother, and settled in Boston.)

When Hodler came to Geneva, it was the only city in nineteenth-century Switzerland boasting an active contemporary artistic culture, animated mainly by François Diday and Alexandre Calame, Swiss landscape painters active in Geneva in the early half of the century but renowned throughout Switzerland. But Hodler was more drawn to Karl Vogt, whom he knew by reputation, a great naturalist who taught geology, paleontology, and zoology at the University of Geneva and who ultimately became its rector. Vogt, who before emigrating to Switzerland had been active in liberal politics in pre-1848 Germany, was able to give the young Hodler some contact with the world of the mind.

While engaged in making copies at the Musée Rath, Hodler encountered Barthélemy Menn, an accomplished painter who really became the artist's teacher. Menn, born in Geneva in 1815 and very influential in the artistic culture there, had studied with Ingres and had gone to Rome with the master. Later on, he also became a friend of Delacroix, Corot, and Daubigny. Menn painted carefully balanced, intimate landscapes with soft contours and high tonalities. Menn, like his teacher Ingres, believed in the primacy of line and structural form. Hodler, coming from a rural environment, was able to enter the great French classic tradition thanks to the six years he worked with Menn as a student in the Ecole des Beaux-Arts in Geneva.

While a student with Menn, Hodler painted one of his earliest self-portraits, *The Student*. In the course of his life Hodler painted at least forty self-portraits, constantly exploring his own image, searching for the key to the deeper meaning of his face and gesture. This self-portrait, done when he was twenty-one, is remarkable for its clear construction: the tall figure occupies the center of the narrow, vertical space; all the parts of the body are based on linear directions and their relationships. A contemporary critic, seeing this painting in an exhibition of the Société Suisse des Beaux-Arts in Geneva in 1876, made the acute observation that "Hodler makes us aware of the epidermis, the weight and the cubic form of his subjects."[1] In this portrait the artist sees himself as a young student with books and canvases in the background. In his left hand he holds a T-square in perfect balance which must signify the interest he took in science and construction. His right hand is raised in an oath and his earnest countenance speaks cogently of his dedication to his life as an artist. But the oath also seems tenuous, the young man's posture is questioning, the expression is still uncertain. Hodler painted his image down to above the knees, probably in order to achieve the desired verticality of the composition; but what a strange place to truncate the figure!

Soon after painting *The Student* Hodler's interest in linear structures, the placement of the figure, and balanced composition, was reinforced by his encounter with Holbein's work

1. *The Student*. 1874. Oil on canvas.
   44½ x 28¾″. Kunsthaus Zurich.

during a visit to Basel. Holbein and Dürer, whose works he was to copy and whose theories were to occupy his mind, were the artists of the North whom Hodler admired most throughout his life. Yet he had equal regard for Michelangelo, Leonardo, and Raphael, whose *Miraculous Draft of the Fishes* he considered "perhaps the most beautiful composition an artist ever made."[2] Although his Symbolist work must be counted among the major breakthroughs of Post-Impressionism, Hodler, like the somewhat older Cézanne, was firmly grounded in tradition, creating a new present with the values of the past.

Hodler continued working with no tangible success. In 1878 he was impelled to move, and suddenly left Geneva for Madrid. Although Florentine masters of the Italian Renaissance remained Hodler's heroes, rather than Titian, Velazquez, and Ribera whose work he encountered in the Prado, the sheer physical dimensions of their paintings must have had great impact on the artist, who, having begun with small landscapes, was to become one of the great muralists of his time.

Watchmaker Workshop Madrid, made during his stay in Madrid, is a very small painting. Here he put three men carefully into a room, placing all objects and figures along a perpendicular structure. This rigorously constructed simple interior, facing the light of a window whose rectangular transparent panes give a view of a bright outside world, relates the Swiss painter to the tradition of German Romantic painting, going back to such artists as Caspar David Friedrich and Georg Kersting, who also created moods of silent intimacy in their Biedermeier interiors. It is fascinating that during a trip to Spain Hodler should relate to North German artists of the early nineteenth century.

3. *Watchmaker Workshop Madrid.* (1879).
Oil on canvas. 32½ x 36⅝″. Kunstmuseum
Lucerne (extended loan from Gottfried
Keller Foundation).

19

Hodler's style was by no means crystallized at this time. In *On the Shore of the Manzanares River near Madrid*, also painted during the first half of 1879, he achieved a fresh, unfinished quality, in complete contrast to that demonstrated in *Watchmaker Workshop Madrid*. This outdoor scene, willow trees on the banks of the small Manzanares River outside Madrid, is filled with sunlight and transmits the airy experience of a bright spring morning. Hodler's knowledge of Corot's landscapes (the rough, airy, and light quality of a painting like *The Bridge at Narni* comes to mind) was transmitted to him by Menn, and suffices, together with the actual experience of the river on this particular day, to explain the seeming influence of Sisley and the Impressionists—work that Hodler had not yet necessarily seen.[3] The Manzanares landscape is the first to break with more traditional ties. Hodler tells us that Menn freed him from conventional ties and "made it his task to restore me to a state of nature and to make me capable of seeing."[4]

4. *On the Shore of the Manzanares River near Madrid.* (1879). Oil on canvas. 17⅜ x 25⅝''. Musée d'Art et d'Histoire, Geneva.

In the summer of 1879 Hodler left Madrid to return to Geneva. Two years later his visage, marked by anger and energy, confronts us in another self-portrait, *The Angry One*. The artist shows himself as having been interrupted, having just turned about to query the intruding viewer with surprise, but also with a speculating and suspicious glance. His glance is direct and seems to emphasize the importance of his own being, and his search for it. In this painting Hodler seems to insist on two aspects of his personality. The left eye in the portrait is startled, terrified, frightened, while the right seems to be threatening and angry, asking the interloper to leave the room. *The Angry One* was the first painting Hodler sent to the Paris Salon (where it was ignored) and also his first work to enter a public collection. The Bern Art Association bought it in 1887 for the city's museum.

5. *The Angry One.* (1881). Oil on canvas.
   28½ x 20¾″. Kunstmuseum Bern.

23

During the ensuing years Hodler participated in all sorts of competitions and managed to win occasional prizes. Yet his financial situation remained desperate, and in Geneva the critical reception of his work was generally negative. He rented a studio in a garret on the Grand'Rue in the oldest quarter of the city and enjoyed the friendship of a number of fellow painters and writers. During the summers he would go back to the Bernese Oberland to paint landscapes which retained the high key of the Spanish interlude and developed an ever greater clarity of structure. In 1885 he painted the superb *Portrait of Louise-Delphine Duchosal*, the young sister of his friend, the poet Louis Duchosal. The composition with the girl sitting straight as a rail in her chair, the placement of the figure against a neutral background of grays, the empty shape created between the girl and the chair, the gesture of tenderly holding a white narcissus, her magnificently painted face, all make this an extraordinary painting. This small canvas, done under the conscious influence of Manet, is infinitely superior to Hodler's ambitious allegorical portrayals in minute detail of athletic festivals or to the historical subject of Calvin and other religious reformers walking the cloisters of the College of Geneva.

8. *Portrait of Louise-Delphine Duchosal.*
   (1885). Oil on canvas. 21⅝ x 18⅛″.
   Kunsthaus Zurich.

In 1885 Hodler also painted a landscape, *Beech Forest*, which must be regarded as the first example of his Parallelism. Parallelism as seen in Hodler's work was a compositional device based on the repetition of similar elements and their relationship to each other. As Hodler explains Parallelism, it is a "principle of order," inherent in nature, reflecting the underlying harmony of creation. Hodler was less concerned with diversity than with universality and unity. Human beings, trees, mountains, are more alike than they are different. "We know and we all feel at times that what unites us is stronger than what divides us."[7]

In his lecture, "Mission of the Artist," delivered at the University of Fribourg in 1897, he explained:

> If I go for a walk in a forest of very high fir trees, I can see ahead of me, to the right and to the left, those innumerable columns formed by the tree trunks. I am surrounded by the same vertical line repeated an infinite number of times. Whether those tree trunks stand out clear against a darker background or whether they are silhouetted against a deep blue sky, the main note, causing that impression of unity, is the parallelism of the trunks.[8]

The painting of the beech forest seems to embody Hodler's statement articulated twelve years later in his Fribourg lecture. In great contrast to the contemporary French Impressionists, fascinated with the accidental quality of their corner of reality, Hodler selected details of nature which limited and in fact delineated his principle. And having found his perfect model, as it were, he emphasized the alignment of the tree trunks, placing them as parallel vertical lines to demonstrate a categorical quality of rhythmic repetition.

9. *Beech Forest.* 1885. Oil on canvas. 39¾ x
51½″. Museum der Stadt Solothurn.

In 1884 Hodler met Augustine Dupin, his close companion for several years, who bore his son Hector in 1887. Hodler painted a number of intimate pictures of mother and child in their home surroundings, small-scale paintings which, unlike his more ambitious compositions, continued the kind of work he did in the portrait of Mlle. Duchosal. *Mother and Child* is a sensitive painting of the mother feeding her little son. Almost like a traditional madonna and child, this painting is very self-contained in its triangular structure. The relationship of color areas such as Hector's red dress, the mother's gray shirt, the nearly black areas of her skirt, hair, and the firescreen, the flesh-colored sections of both figures as well as the brown semi-elipse of the table, make an abstract pattern of interacting shapes that is not accidental but which helps create the feeling of closeness between mother and child. The treatment of color and composition in this painting recalls the portraits by Degas.

It is very likely that by this time Hodler was familiar with Degas' work, probably through Marcellin Desboutin, who had been Degas' close friend and who was on familiar terms with the French cultural elite, including Degas' friends, the Viscount Lepic and Henri Rouart, as well as Puvis de Chavannes, Courbet, Renoir, Morisot, George Sand, Emile Zola, and Dumas fils. Desboutin was a playwright, collector, and etcher of portraits, and, while carefully maintaining his contacts in Paris, settled in Geneva in the early 1870s. Hodler's contact with Desboutin must have been important, because it enabled him to become familiar with French artists whom his teacher, Barthélemy Menn, could not have known. Walter Hugelshofer points out: "In Desboutin, Paris came to Hodler."[9] It was conceivable that due to Desboutin's encouragement Hodler sent more of his work to exhibitions in Paris. At the World's Fair of 1889 he received an honorable mention for his large, ponderous composition, *Procession of Wrestlers.*

12. *Mother and Child.* (ca. 1889). Oil on canvas. 14⅛×11″. Collection Professor Hans R. Hahnloser, Bern.

The painting that gained him international recognition, however, was *Night*, which he began with few prior studies in 1889 and completed in 1890. Here for the first time Hodler uses the human figure, as well as color and light, to create a symbolic Parallelist painting. The Parallelism created by the extended horizontal figures is clearly emphasized by areas of light and dark—bodies and their garments—that form a domino pattern throughout the painting. Leaving narrative painting behind, Hodler achieves a work which no longer describes an event but rather evokes a feeling. *Night* suggests a unique fusion of eros, sleep, and death.

Six of the eight figures in the composition are asleep. As in a dream, the stagelike space is crowded. Some of the figures are modeled after people close to Hodler's life, while others are related more directly to art. The woman who sleeps alone on the lower left with her body covered and her knees, feet, and elbows crossed in a position of closure is his friend Augustine Dupin. The sensuous and seductive nude embracing a young man on the lower right is not his new wife, Berta Stucki, with whom Hodler lived only about as long as he worked on this major composition. The figure on the upper right, which certainly appears to be another self-portrait, resembles the lying Diogenes in the center of Raphael's *School of Athens* (a point also made by von Tavel in his book on *Night*). It is highly significant that in the very painting which marks the turning point in Hodler's work toward the future, the "most important painting, in which I reveal myself in a new light,"[10] Hodler reaches back to the world of the Italian Renaissance. It is not only Raphael, but also Michelangelo's Medici tombs and Signorelli's *Pan* which come to mind when confronted by this major work. The central figure is the artist, who had known death so well throughout his early life, suddenly awakened and terrified by a black hooded figure. The message is clear. To make it even more so, Hodler wrote on the frame: "Plus d'un qui s'est couché tranquillement le soir, ne s'éveillera pas le lendemain matin." Yet what a strange image of death: it appears here as a seducer, crouched implacably on the artist's genitals. His attempt to push this threatening figure away from him seems to be of no avail. This painting clearly recalls the eighteenth-century Swiss canvas, Fuseli's famous *Nightmare*,[11] in which an incubus, a sneering demon, crouches on the chest of the sleeping figure of a sensuously entranced girl. But instead of the enigmatic, provocative, and feverish eroticism of Fuseli's pantomime, Hodler, a century later, deals with the nightmare of sex and death in measured rhythm and symmetry.

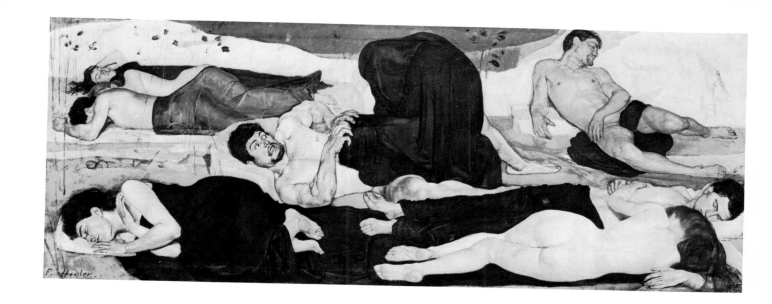

14. *Night.* (1890). Oil on canvas. 45¾ x 117¾".
Kunstmuseum Bern.

Henry Johann Heinrich Fuseli (Switzerland,
1741–1825). *The Nightmare.* (1790–1971).
Oil on canvas. Goethe Museum, Frankfurt
am Main, Germany. [Not in exhibition.]

In 1891 *Night* was withdrawn from the municipal exhibition at the order of Geneva's mayor. Hodler then exhibited the painting most successfully at his own expense, in a space he rented elsewhere in the city. Hodler sent it to the Salon du Champ-de-Mars, where it was received enthusiastically and admired by Puvis de Chavannes. The artist himself traveled to Paris and was elected a member of the Société National des Artistes Français. Joséphin (Sâr) Péladan, founder of the Rose†Croix Esthétique and for a brief time very influential in cultural matters, called the picture "unforgettable, a work of art which bespeaks a great future."[12] In 1892 the painting was shown officially in Bern and in 1897 it (along with Hodler's *Eurythmy*) was awarded the coveted gold medal at the VII International Art Exhibition in Munich. In 1899 it was sent to the III Biennale in Venice and the following year it was again in Paris, this time at the World's Fair, where it (with *Eurythmy* and *Day*) received a gold medal, and Hodler's reputation as a modern master was established. In 1901 *Night* was finally purchased, together with three other major works, by the Bern Kunstmuseum.

One of these works was another large symbolic canvas, *The Disillusioned*, which was sent to Paris almost immediately upon its completion in 1892. In fact, Count Antoine de La Roche-foucauld, financial backer of the Rose†Croix Esthétique, traveled to Geneva to invite Hodler to exhibit this new work in Paris in the first salon of this heterogeneous group of painters, at Durand-Ruel's in March 1892. Although Péladan's pronouncements were very doctrinaire, the many divergent talents exhibited in the Salon included not only followers of Puvis, Moreau, and Gauguin, but also Redon and Toorop, all of whom shared an anti-Impressionist and anti-contemporary point of view and were perhaps in some sort of agreement with the Sâr's neo-Catholic metaphysics. Certainly Hodler belonged to a new group of artists who considered nature only a source which would help to symbolize emotion. Like his great contemporaries Gauguin, Van Gogh, Munch, or Ensor, Ferdinand Hodler saw in art a means toward edification rather than mere delectation.

17. *The Disillusioned.* 1892. Oil on canvas.
47¼ x 117¾″. Kunstmuseum Bern.

33

The Disillusioned represents five old men sitting on a bench, having renounced their struggle, accepting the inevitable fate of old age in silent despair. Although this painting may be based on sketches Hodler made of men sitting on the benches of the parks of Geneva, these figures in their timeless garments are an allegory of human despondency and desolation rather than a realistic rendition. Two darkly garbed figures on the left correspond to two on the right, while the central figure differs in dress and posture. The repetition and axial symmetry carry the message that this is not a fortuitous grouping of men, but a carefully arranged symbolic representation of man's fate. The repetition frees these men from solitude and creates a symbolic human community. The clear and emphatic contour lines, the vertical lines of the men, the horizontal one of the bench—everything is placed on a shallow, stagelike space. Although the figures are copied from nature (Hodler must have had his models seated in the positions in which they are portrayed), he joined the leading post-Impressionist painters in emphasis on the picture plane, in free and symbolic use of color and line, and above all in the identity of form and idea. No wonder, then, that Hodler was taken up with enthusiasm by the Symbolists and Nabis of Paris. Félix Vallotton, a younger Swiss compatriot and a member of the Rose † Croix Esthétique, reported from Paris in the *Gazette de Lausanne* of March 18, 1892, that he found the five figures "powerfully restrained in black and white against the rose-colored background of a hill truly unforgettable" and commented further that it would be necessary to go "far back into the past, to the frescoes of Orcagna and Signorelli, to find such power of drawing, such dignity of form."

Ferdinand Hodler painting "The Disillu-
sioned" near the cemetery of St. Georges at
Geneva (1892). [Photo by Marc Odier,
Geneva, courtesy Jura Brüschweiler, ©].

18. *Disillusioned One.* 1892. Oil on canvas.
21¾ x 17½". Collection B. Gerald Cantor,
Beverly Hills, California.

The rhythmic arrangement of parallel figures, with a central one differentiated from the pairs on left and right in a shallow frontal plane, is repeated in *Eurythmy* (1894–1895). This was one of Hodler's favorite paintings, "because of its simplicity, its large parallels, its white garments with their simple folds that make delicate ornaments at the man's feet."[13] In this picture, Hodler breaks the stasis of his former large figural compositions and introduces rhythmic movements by the motion of the figures themselves. Five old men, whose faces recall those of Dürer's *Four Apostles* in Munich (a likeness pointed out by Ewald Bender), are dressed in festive, white loose-fitting robes. They move fluidly from left to right, from life toward death.[14] The figures, consuming almost all of the space, are monumental in appearance. Hodler's Parallelism, which expresses his metaphysical vision, may remind us of the hieratic frieze of saints in Sant' Apollinare Nuovo, with the measured rhythms created by the procession of saints and virgins. Yet the fluidity of the movement is distinct from the static ritual enacted at Ravenna. In his Fribourg lecture, Hodler speaks of the artist "searching for the linear beauty of a contour," "stressing the movements and the parts of the human body," "expressing its rhythm," and he explains further that "the outline of the human body changes according to its movements and is in itself an element of beauty."[15]

In this attitude Hodler closely approaches new ideas in dance which developed during his lifetime. The figures in a great many of Hodler's large symbolic compositions after 1890 assume the stance of modern dancers.[16] (His biographer and student, Stephanie Guerzoni, tells how he worked directly from dancing models.)[17] During the last decade of the century, it must be remembered, art increasingly moved toward the non-discursive condition of music and dance. In this respect, his later friendship with Emile Jacques Dalcroze, a distinguished musicologist, choreographer, and professor at the Geneva conservatory of music, was also important. One of the great innovators of the modern dance movement, Dalcroze was indebted to Loïé Fuller and Isadora Duncan and taught eurythmics long before Rudolf Steiner. There is little doubt that Hodler saw Dalcroze's performances, that he supported the younger man's work and was, in turn, inspired by it, particularly by Dalcroze's exercises with successive movements. When Hodler died Dalcroze wrote a moving obituary; ten years later in an article entitled "Ferdinand Hodler et le Rhythm," he stated that "the principal inspiration in Hodler's work was rhythm, . . . his painting appears eminently musical in the Greek sense of the word." Seeing "rhythm and meter as the foundation of art," Dalcroze continues: "This continuous preoccupation with movement is just made to interest musicians. Hodler is certainly one of them. None of them better than he possess the art of associating and disassociating movements, of accenting unisons, of creating counterpoint, of treating human sentiments symphonically, of choosing for their expression the gestures and positions appropriate for their orchestration."[18]

22. *Eurythmy.* 1895. Oil on canvas. 65¾ x 96½".
Kunstmuseum Bern.

But long before Hodler's acquaintance with Dalcroze, we find that dream-like movements and ritual gestures animate his figures and give them their symbolic significance and psychological content. Even seated figures—the five old men in *The Disillusioned* or the five young women in *Day*, indeed even recumbent figures like the couples in *Love*—are articulated by the heightened stage gestures of mimes or dancers. Frequently Hodler's large figures, whether standing, sitting, or lying, are static and at complete rest, but even the walking men in *Eurythmy* move in measured steps through frozen time and space. It is certainly this use of the seemingly static and overstated gesture that over the years has been the source of much critical objection to Hodler's stylizations. But it is precisely the measured gesture of his hieratic figures which evoke the viewer's reaction along the lines determined by this Symbolist painter.

Symbolism and Art Nouveau, movements in which Hodler participated at the turn of the century, are characterized in painting by the evocative use of flat linear form and, "Like his Art Nouveau contemporaries, Hodler worked in terms of the plane enriched with a decorative pattern, where a tense line becomes the important carrier of emotion."[19] This trend becomes most apparent in *Day* of 1899–1900. Here the five figures are seated on a flatly patterned mountain meadow in a linear dancelike movement. Again the Parallelist composition consists of a central figure flanked symmetrically by two figures on each side. Their gestures are repeated in the rising hill in the background, if indeed we can still speak of a background in so flat a composition. The young women are nude, and the theme of daybreak is developed in their bodies and movements. The two on the outer edge of the painting have their legs in a guarded and closed position while their arms are folded as in prayer. They are introverted figures. The two women next to them turn more directly toward the viewer, but while their thighs are more open, their arms almost hide their faces in an averting gesture. The severe central figure with her arms in a gesture of open prayer appears like a priestess who channels the emotion of the group toward the light of day. If *Night* was a painting to symbolize the threat of death, *Day* is a hymn to awakening and light.

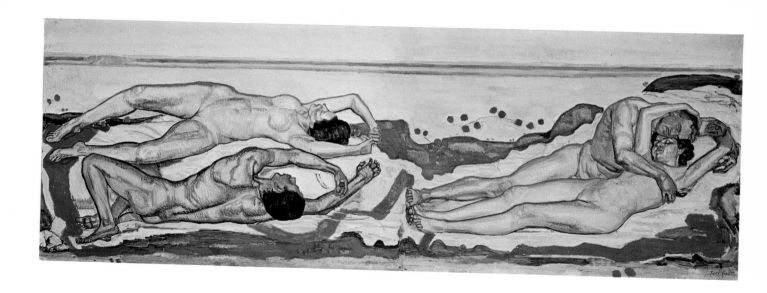

Love. Oil on panel. Collection Josef Müller,
Solothurn. [Not in exhibition.]

26. *Day II.* (1904–1906). Oil on canvas. 64¼ x
141″. Kunsthaus Zurich.

Truth, painted in 1903, when Hodler spent six weeks in Vienna and became a friend and admirer of Gustav Klimt and the Jugendstil artists of the Vienna Secession, combines the decorative arabesque with allegorical meaning. Strained and contorted figures standing on a stylized meadow fuse with the surface of the picture. A nude woman with arms outstretched symmetrically stands in the center, banishing the six half-draped demons at her side. Unlike Klimt and many of his Art Nouveau contemporaries, Hodler does not treat woman as a languidly sensuous decorative object. The slender young girl here is seen as the liberator, the symbol of the good and the true, while the men with faces covered and averted are unable to bear the vision of naked Truth which stands before them. It is the male figures who are partly draped in an almost provocative manner, while Truth herself—we are reminded somehow of Titian's allegory of love—is completely naked and pure. Color is used to emphasize the meaning, which is surely the victory of light and day over the dark and morbid forces of the night.

A few years later, in his magnificent composition, *Love*, the artist has moved beyond the allegorical decoration of Jugendstil. Stylizations and mannerisms are rejected in favor of a deeply felt realistic rendition of the human form. On a long, ribbon-like, horizontal canvas three couples are stretched out like waves at the edge of the sea. Rarely has his use of color been more forceful and meaningful, and never has he painted the human body more masterfully. It seems as if all the problems and threats and fears of *Night* have now been resolved in this painting of frankly assertive physical love. If the couples in *Night* were meant to symbolize death, the three couples in this large mural are images of life, of the completion of passion and love. This painting has an elemental power lacking in his more symbolic compositions. Parallelism is no longer a matter of doctrine at this point, but appears in the natural and easy flow of three couples embracing at the edge of the sea.

25. *Truth II.* (1903). Oil on canvas. 81⅞x116⅛″.
Kunsthaus Zurich.

With the exception of *Love*, there is generally a heavy and didactic element in Hodler's large compositions symbolizing the human condition. They seem to be done by a painter different from Hodler the landscapist. His landscapes, mostly pictures of mountains, are done with much greater freedom and spontaneity. Yet, especially in his landscapes executed before the turn of the century, we find similar uses of parallel structure and similar attitudes toward the meaning of color. "Color has a penetrating, harmonious charm, independent of form. It influences emotions. . ." and Hodler goes on to explain that we associate certain colors with certain feelings. White, for instance, "usually means purity."[20] *Eurythmy* is predominantly a white painting. His beautiful landscape of 1892, *Autumn Evening*, is composed of golden browns. The painting is unified in its color scheme; there is no aerial perspective, but instead a completely even color intensity. In order to give the landscape a universal and motionless aspect, he has suppressed the presence of figures and painted over the original female figure walking on the road. In his search for parallel structure in nature, Hodler now rejects totally the transitory quality of the Impressionist landscape. The composition is symmetrical. The chestnut trees, moreover, are not shown growing naturally and at random, but have been arranged so as to infuse man's order into nature. The absence of shadows adds to the austere quality of this structural landscape. The avenue is greatly foreshortened, moving rapidly to its vanishing point. Yet for all its measure and structure—and this is perhaps the essential aspect of this fine landscape—the road itself not only goes into the sunset, it leads into infinity, to the immeasurable. The leaves fall aimlessly, announcing the approach of winter.

Hodler's desire for measure within his pantheist awe of the boundless universe seems almost analogous to the sentiment of the great Symbolist poet Rainer Maria Rilke:

Fall
The leaves are falling, falling from afar
as though far gardens withered in the skies;
they fall with constantly denying gestures.

And in the night the heavy earth is falling
from all the stars into its loneliness.

We all are falling. This hand falls,
and look at others: it is in them all.

And yet there is One, who holds this falling
in his own hands with timeless tenderness.[21]

16. *Autumn Evening.* (1892). Oil on canvas.
39⅜ x 51¼". Musée d'Art et d'Histoire,
Neuchatel.

The symmetry of *Autumn Evening* is a quality Hodler retained in landscapes for some time. Often, instead of using a vertical axis, he orients his landscapes on a horizontal one. For the remainder of his life, he painted many views of Lake Geneva, often as seen from Chexbres or Vevey. He would look down at the expanse of the lake and make a large oval form in which the near shore is echoed by the sweep of the mountains on the far side, while clouds in the sky are reflected in the waters of the lake. In *Lake Geneva from Chexbres* of 1895, a high sweeping cloud formation repeats the defining curve of the near shoreline. Hodler combines a sense of realism and place with his theoretical principle of Parallelism. The numerous variations of the wide view of Lake Geneva attest the constant refinement of his vision.

23. *Lake Geneva from Chexbres.* (1895). Oil
on canvas. 39⅜ x 51¼″. Kunsthaus Zurich
(extended loan from Gottfried Keller
Foundation).

57. *Sunset at Lake Geneva.* (1915). Oil on
canvas. 24x35½″. Kunsthaus Zurich.

29. *Lake Geneva from Chexbres.* (1906-1908).
Oil on canvas. 31½x50¾″. Collection Kurt
Meissner, Zurich.

67. *The Shore of Lake Geneva at Dawn.*
(1918). Oil on canvas. 24⅛x50⅜″. Musée
d'Art et d'Histoire, Geneva.

During the summer months Hodler also often returned to Lake Thun, where he had worked with Ferdinand Sommer when he was a very young man, to paint a series of landscapes. One of the later of these is *Lake Thun* of 1909. This painting is almost a schematic example of double axial symmetry with the far shoreline again serving as the central horizontal axis, while the waves in the lake create a repeat pattern of parallel lines. In addition, the mountains beyond the lake rise in a symmetrical manner around an invisible vertical axis. To an eye accustomed to the charming random quality of an Impressionist landscape, this painting may appear too stylized and theoretical, but Hodler was well aware of his purpose. In 1904, during his great triumph in Vienna, he remarked that "when I began, I turned toward Impressionism. Slowly, however, due to study and years of observation, I came into my current trend: *clear form, simple representation, repetition of motifs.*"[22] Similarly, Heinrich Wölfflin, a great admirer of Hodler, felt that "to a certain extent he brought the accidental together into a universal order."[23]

36. *Lake Thun.* 1909. Oil on canvas. 26½ x
36¼". Musée d'Art et d'Histoire, Geneva.

On a trip to the Engadin in 1907, Hodler painted *Lake Silvaplana* on a bright, crystal-clear day. To achieve harmony and unity in this painting of the high mountain lake, he again paints the image of the mountains reflected perfectly in the water. The banks, which in actuality are more parallel, seem to run together in a horizontal line, forming the wide shoreline across the lake. The mountains on the left side are echoed on the right, but this painting goes far beyond the scheme of double symmetry. The colors in *Lake Silvaplana*, the reddish brown of the mountains, the emerald green of the meadows, the clear blue of sky and water make this painting a superb image of nature.

Lake Silvaplana. 1907. Oil on canvas. 28 x 36⅜".
Kunsthaus Zurich. [Not in exhibition.]

Perhaps the crowning achievement of Hodler's landscapes at the turn of the century is *Eiger, Mönch, and Jungfrau in Moonlight* of 1908. Here, in this painting, kept almost entirely in blues, the three great peaks emerge majestically from night fog. The mood is set by the color, the drama is created by light and the relationships of the shapes. Two dark clouds float in the center of the painting and are outlined by cold bright rings of moonlight. They relate to each other as if there were a cosmic charge between them, and they are embraced by a great crescent of clouds high above them. A sense of heavy mystery infuses this nightscape above the partially veiled mountains. The painting suggests a pantheist concept, comparable to that expressed a half-century later by Mark Rothko, who often dealt similarly with floating, luminous shapes impinging on each other. The rhythms created by Hodler's visionary painting seem to correspond to the rhythmic feelings of the artist's innermost self, and are communicated to the viewer. Having abandoned the more dogmatic scheme of Parallelism, Hodler expresses the magical experience and sense of the mountain night more directly. We know that the mountain landscape itself, no matter how beautiful, can never equal the strength of feeling expressed—now almost unconsciously—by the artist's sense of formal structure.

32. *Eiger, Mönch, and Jungfrau in Moonlight.*
 (1908). Oil on canvas. 28⅜x26⅜". Collection Josef Müller, Solothurn.

Hodler frequently went high up into the mountains to come close to the Alpine giants. He would go to the Schynige Platte, to Grindelwald or Mürren to be as close as possible to the great Jungfrau massif so he could study and paint the grandiose quality of the mountains, or he would paint the solitary Niesen, which stands like a pyramid against the sky. *Niesen* of 1910 was painted in broad brushstrokes; Hodler was interested in the flat decorative pattern of convoluted clouds above the equilateral triangle of the peak. A year later, discarding Art Nouveau ornamentation, he painted a monumental picture, the *Breithorn*, in pure blues, whites and browns. The mountain is outlined in hard, defined contour lines, the masses are carefully balanced. The rocks beneath the snow are brought out in very sharp and clear relief. In fact, Hodler uses somewhat lighter tones for the foreground of these pictures and darker values for the distance, reversing the traditional means of treating landscapes. Thus, by denying aerial perspective, he achieves the two-dimensional effect he wants and brings the mountain close to the viewer. In these pictures he reveals the architectural structure of the object—and this is the essence of his modernity here. His friend, the noted Swiss painter Cuno Amiet expressed: "Hodler seems to me to be more of an architect than a painter."[24]

38. *Niesen.* (1910). Oil on canvas. 32¾ x 41½".
Oeffentliche Kunstsammlung Basel.

The artist himself underplayed the importance of his magnificent landscapes, viewing them as a summer relaxation from the work he considered truly significant, and, since there was now an enormous demand for these pictures, as a means to make money. This is clear from the following remark: "People think I'm all out for money. If that were so, I'd have to paint only landscapes, which sell like hot cakes. The figures are the only important things for me."[25] Contemporary criticism, however, did not agree: "The landscapes of Hodler are as significant and independent as the landscapes by Cézanne and Van Gogh. It could easily happen that the history of art of the future will elevate Hodler the landscapist above the master of monumental style."[26]

This has indeed happened to a considerable extent. Hodler's feeling for the monumental seemed to a good many critics more suited to the depiction of the mountain than to the representation of man, perhaps because Hodler's sense of the stasis and immobility with which he endows his large figure compositions disturbs critics possessed of a more realistic sensibility. And mountains, after all, are about as solid and permanent as anything can be. In his paintings of lone summits or Alpine massifs, Hodler went far beyond depicting individual mountains; he came close to creating a universal symbol of the concept MOUNTAIN. It is astonishingly true that nobody had ever painted the Alps with such deep understanding of the solitude that reigns among the peaks or of the powerful quality of rock and ravine, gorge and glacier. Earlier painters of mountains might offer a sublime, romantic, inner-directed vision like that of Caspar David Friedrich, or they might idealize the Alps with a sense of classical order and Arcadian nostalgia, as did Josef Anton Koch and his followers. The Impressionists painted mountains with a soft lyricism. Hodler's Swiss predecessors and contemporaries (with a few exceptions, such as Giovanni Giacometti, Cuno Amiet, and Giovanni Segantini) were generally satisfied with sentimentally picturesque views of the Alps.

41. *Breithorn*. (1911). Oil on canvas. 26⅜x35".
Kunstmuseum Lucerne (extended loan
from Bernhard Eglin Foundation).

In his late landscapes Hodler becomes increasingly free. A painting like *Landscape near Caux with Rising Clouds* of 1917 no longer has any sharp contours and there is little structured composition. Everything is dissolved into light and color in this remarkable painting from the summits. Years later René Daumal in a visionary novel, *Mount Analogue*, tells about a mountain painter: "She understands that the view one has from a high peak is not registered in the same perceptive range as a still life or an ordinary landscape. The paintings admirably express the circular structure of space in the upper regions."[27]

Aware of the special feeling he achieved with his late landscapes, Hodler himself referred to them, perhaps jokingly, as "paysages planétaires." During the last months of his life, no longer able to go up to his retreat at Montreux, he finally could not even leave his apartment to go to his studio. He then stood at his window at the Quai de Mont Blanc in Geneva and painted a series of landscapes, at all times of day and in all weather, of the wide lake, the Mont Blanc massif, and the sky.

Painted with loose brushwork, these pictures are mostly in blue and gold. They are small; some are bright and crisp in color, others dark and glowing. They are very horizontal and emphasize the width of the lake flowing by like a river, the mountains, and the sky—the three elements so important to Hodler's experience. They symbolize the visible world, and they become increasingly abstract. Shortly before he died, Hodler stood on the banks of Lake Geneva with Johannes Widmer and said: "I want to paint different landscapes now, or paint my landscapes differently. Do you see how over there everything is dissolved into lines and space? Don't you feel as if you were standing at the edge of the earth and were able to communicate freely with the universe? That's how I want to paint from now on."[28]

62. *Landscape near Caux with Rising Clouds.*
1917. Oil on canvas. 25¾x31⅞″. Kunsthaus
Zurich.

In many ways Hodler felt as if he were "standing at the edge." When he was seven years old his father died. At fourteen he experienced the slow dying of his mother, also of tuberculosis. "We were miserably poor then and the funeral was as paltry as possible," Hodler recalls. "The raw wooden coffin was put on a simple pushcart and the funeral cortege consisted of us children, my brothers, sister and myself stumbling behind it. This picture has remained light and clear in front of my eyes during my whole life."[29]

The deaths of both parents were followed in rapid succession by the deaths of most of his brothers and his sister. "In the family there was constant dying. It seemed to me as if Death were always in the house, as if this is how it had to be,"[30] Hodler remembers, speaking also of the permanence of death.

After his arrival in Geneva as a young man, he was permitted by Karl Vogt to draw and study corpses in the dissecting room of the University, and in 1876, soon after seeing Hans Holbein's great *Dead Christ* in Basel, he painted two intense canvases: *Woman on Her Deathbed* and *Dead Man*. Years later, when his ideas crystallized, he painted *Night*, the most decisive work of his career; it is an allegory of death. Many of the symbolic compositions that followed dealt with termination of life. *The Disillusioned* have reached the end of existence. *Eurythmy* deals with the inevitable walk toward oblivion. In this respect Hodler's sensitivity relates him closely to his contemporary, Edvard Munch, who had similar early experiences with death in his family. Moreover, at the fin-de-siècle a preoccupation with death and the meaning of life was general among painters, sculptors, poets, playwrights, and novelists, and Hodler was very much a man of his time.

Even in his historic compositions, paintings often meant to celebrate heroic exploits of Swiss warriors, Hodler chooses to deal with tragedy, defeat, and death: the mural, *The Retreat from Marignano*, was commissioned for the Hall of Armor at the Schweizerisches Landesmuseum in Zurich. It commemorates the retreat of the Swiss army at Marignano early in the sixteenth century. *The Wounded Warrior* of 1897 is a full-scale color sketch for the Zurich mural. The standard-bearer has rescued the flag on which he still leans, about to succumb to the wounds of battle. The greatest of his historical compositions, and probably Hodler's chef d'oeuvre—the large mural celebrating *The Departure of the Volunteers in 1813* at the University of Jena—depicts the steady march of soldiers, moving irresistibly into battle, facing inevitable death.

24. *Wounded Warrior.* (1897). Oil on canvas.
78½ x 68⅞". Musée d'Art et d'Historie,
Geneva.

Beginning with the portrait *The Poet Louis Duchosal on His Deathbed* in 1901, Hodler recorded the death of those close to him with agonizing precision. In 1909 Augustine Dupin, his former mistress and mother of his son Hector, became seriously ill, and the artist went to her, stayed with her, and recorded her sickness and death, always adding the exact date to his signature. The final painting, *Augustine Dupin on Her Deathbed*, painted the day after she died, has the name "Hodler" added to hers: Augustine was finally acknowledged by her lover. The thin woman in black with hands folded is stretched out, stiff and immobile. Death is expressed by prostrate horizontality, which is reiterated by three parallel blue lines painted high on the ochre wall above the dead woman. Hodler told Hans Mühlestein that they stood for the soul of the deceased[31] They certainly bring the concept of Parallelism into the realm of abstract symbolism. To Hodler, the permanence and universality of death was the final manifestation of unity among all people.

In an excellent essay on Hodler's Augustine Dupin death cycle, Jura Brüschweiler comments on this last of the four paintings:

...Now the body is totally collapsed and stiffened in its definitive horizontality. It lies like a wave that becomes immobile before disappearing at the shore of destiny. "Mountains become lower and more rounded by the centuries until they become as flat as the surface of water," Hodler said about nature. By dramatically foreshortening Augustine's corpse, the painter rediscovers this tendency of forms to dissolve into horizontality. The corpse, clothed in a black dress which sparkles with specks of royal blue and bottle green that are reminiscent of life, lies on a white bed streaked with bluish-gray and olive-gray. Enclosed between the lateral edges of the painting, Augustine seems smaller. Her rigid hands have been crossed over her stomach and her feet point upward in a grotesquely maladroit fashion. Hooded by her green-black hair, in curls now tipped white, Augustine's relaxed face has been finely modeled in tones of white, ochre and yellow chalk. Death, in one of its pitiless paradoxes, has restored an air of youth to her, only to petrify it in an inanimate mask. The wall in back of Augustine not only occupies three-fourths of the painting: it suggests infinite space. It is given rhythm by three large, tormented strokes; these appear as the emanation of the soul, which is exhaled and condensed into three nocturnal clouds. In this elevated echo of the horizontal rhythm of death, Hodler's Parallelism goes beyond all decorative intention to attain a cosmic significance. This final vision of Augustine is the masterpiece of the cycle[32]

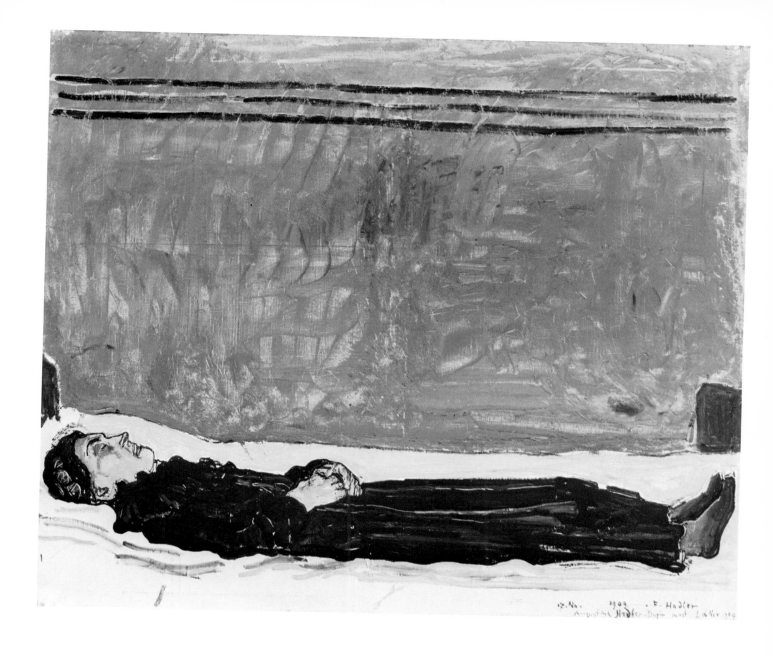

35. *Augustine Dupin on her Deathbed.* 1909. Oil
on canvas. 29¾ x 35½″. Museum der Stadt
Solothurn (Dübi-Müller Foundation).

Several years later Hodler once more became completely absorbed in the theme of death, or, as he called it, "the permanence of absence."[33] He was about fifty-five when he met the woman to whom he came closest in his life: Valentine Godé-Darel, a well-educated woman from Paris who came to Geneva in her thirties and became Hodler's model, his intimate friend, and the mother of his daughter, Pauline. In 1913 Valentine became ill with cancer and from that point to her death in 1915, Hodler went to her sickbed near Lausanne, day after day. There he made a great many drawings and paintings as well as his only sculpture of the sick, the dying, and the dead Mme. Godé-Darel, whose dignity he compared to that of a Byzantine empress.[34] This cycle is fully documented and analyzed by Phyllis Hattis in this monograph on the basis of nine drawings.[35] Among the paintings, *The Sick Valentine Godé-Darel*, created in December of 1914, is the most poignant in its eloquence. Here she is stretched out on her bed, her head still at right angles (eventually she will become entirely horizontal), her features finely chiseled, her face clearly defined by pain, her mouth slightly opened, almost as if in the breath of expiration. Her body under the sheets flows on, wavelike. The watch, undoubtedly Hodler's, which is placed against the wall indicates that her time has almost reached its end. And, as if to indicate their close relationship, the artist paints three roses on the wall, a motif he uses in that extraordinary self-portrait of 1914 with the raised eyebrows and cynical glance in the Schaffhausen museum.

Ferdinand Hodler and Valentine Godé-Darel
(ca. 1909). [Photo by C. Ruf, Zurich, courtesy
Jura Brüschweiler, Geneva. ©].

52. *The Sick Valentine Godé-Darel.* 1914. Oil
on canvas. 24¾ x 33½″. Collection Mrs.
Gertrud Dübi, Solothurn.

We have already mentioned that Hodler observed his own countenance and produced a large number of self-portraits. These are concentrated primarily in his early and late years—the years of self-doubt and trouble. They rarely occur during his middle period. But in 1891, fresh from his success in Paris with *Night*, and probably after his trip to the French capital, he painted his own image in the most affirmative and almost aggressive manner. This is an extraordinarily clean, fresh, and direct portrait. The painter turns around to look at the viewer not with the angry and threatened expression seen in *The Angry One*, done ten years earlier, but open and bright. The most remarkable aspect of this forceful self-portrait is the clear, observing eyes—of which Johannes Brahms remarked to the Bern writer Joseph Viktor Widmann: "Have you seen these wonderful eyes glowing with energy and talent? You better go there. Certainly something significant can be expected."[36]

Some twenty years later in the frontal *Self-portrait* in the Winterthur museum, we see the artist still with penetrating and wide open eyes, but now fatigued, confused, and troubled. This self-portrait was created in 1912 at the very peak of his career. Hodler was now invited to participate in almost every major international exhibition, he had one-man shows in Germany, and many important mural commissions from Zurich to Hannover. He was certainly one of the most sought-after artists of his time and had all the financial rewards that come with success. But Augustine Dupin had died, and 1912 marked the beginning of their son Hector's chronic illness. Despite outward success, Hodler seems to look at the mirror with an expression of disappointment as if to say: "Is this all there is?"

Two years later in the *Self-portrait* now in Schaffhausen the expression of disillusionment has given way to a skeptical, cynical, almost suspicious one. Hodler's style has also changed again: instead of the loose brushwork of the 1912 portrait, he works in a much more linear manner, emphasizing the deep folds in his brow, which like an arc relate to the decorative, abstract flowers in the background. The mouth is tightly shut, the whole face has become thinner. As the question of life and its meaning seems to occupy Hodler more profoundly, he searched his own face more intensely and painted no fewer than twenty-three self-portraits during the remaining five years of his life.

In one of the many self-portraits of 1916, Hodler looks at us again with a questioning demeanor, his shirt front and necktie are disheveled now, and there is a look of sadness in the old man's face. Yet—perhaps because he changed the composition of the head—there appears a light halo or nimbus around the distinct contour of the head which adds to this painting's icon-like quality.

51. *Self-portrait.* 1914. Oil on canvas. 16¾ x 15⅛".
Museum zu Allerheiligen Schaffhausen.

59. *Self-portrait.* 1916. Oil on canvas. 15¾ x 15".
Musée d'Art et d'Histoire, Geneva.

47. *Self-portrait.* (1912). Oil on canvas.
13¼ x 10⅝". Kunstmuseum Winterthur.

Finally in the self-portrait of 1917–1918, also in the Geneva museum, he has become a broken man. His friends have died, his financial and artistic success, which had been won with such difficulty, came to an end as his German patrons boycotted him because of his protest against the shelling and partial destruction of Reims Cathedral by the German artillery. He painted his images with a light and loose brush, because his illness no longer left him the strength for more solid painting. Much as in the landscapes of Lake Geneva done at the same time, the color is applied in a thin film of marks and stains instead of in his former, more conventional brushwork. The result is an unfinished, calligraphic, and abstractly vital appearance. But if there appears to be vitality in the brushwork, the face itself with its almost ritual stare and expression of awe has an incorporeal aspect: the artist facing death.

Notes

[1] B. in *Le Petit Genevois*, April 17, 1876, quoted in Jura Brüschweiler, *Ferdinand Hodler*, Lausanne, 1971, p. 16. [2] Fritz Widmann, *Erinnerungen an Ferdinand Hodler*, Zurich, 1918, p. 28. [3] This is suggested by Walter Hugelshofer in his important monograph *Ferdinand Hodler*, Zurich, 1952, pp. 17–18. [4] Hodler, "Barthélemy Menn," Bibliothèque Publique et Universitaire, Geneva, Ms. fr. 1984/273–74 (no title, no date). See the translation of this text in the present catalogue. [5] *Ferdinand Hodler*, exhibition catalogue, Wiener Secession, Vienna, 1962, pp. 37–38 (documentation by Jura Brüschweiler). [6] This painting has always been dated 1890. In fact this date which appears on the canvas is in Hodler's hand. Recent research by Jura Brüschweiler ("La datation du 'Bois des Frères' de F. Hodler et la naissance du parallelisme" in *Musées de Genève*, Nos. 103 and 105, Geneva, March/May 1970) makes it clear, however, that is was actually done in 1885 for the Concours Calame of that year and signed and dated incorrectly by Hodler at a later time. [7] Hodler, "The Mission of the Artist," Fribourg, 1897. See the translation of this text in the present catalogue. [8] *Ibid.* [9] Walter Hugelshofer, *Ferdinand Hodler*, Zurich, 1952. [10] Hodler, "Mes tendances actuelles—'La Nuit,'" (1891), Bibliothèque Publique et Universitaire, Geneva, Ms. fr. 2984/361–66. See the translation of this text in the present catalogue. [11] John Henry Fuseli's *Nightmare*, painted in 1781 a few years after his arrival in London from Zurich, enjoyed tremendous fame all over Europe. Professor Gert Schiff tells me that "although none of the extant copies of this painting were in Switzerland during Hodler's lifetime, the painting was fairly popular on the grounds of innumerable engravings of which Hodler could certainly have seen one" (Schiff, letter to the author, April 4, 1972). The visual evidence certainly makes this familiarity very likely, and it is known that Hodler saw and admired a drawing by the Swiss-English painter. Arnold Federmann, in his earlier monograph of Fuseli, sees "a secret thread connecting Fuseli's work with Hodler's" (*Johann Heinrich Füssli*, Zurich and Leipzig, 1927, p. 70). [12] Joséphin Péladan, *Le Salon (Dixième Année)*, Paris, 1891, pp. 32–33. [13] Hodler in D. Baud-Bovy, "L'Oeuvre de Ferdinand Hodler," *La Tribune*, Geneva, May 27, 1918. [14] Hodler, "Eurythmy: Five men representing humanity, marching toward death," in "Notes Ultimes" (notebook of F. Hodler), 1917–1918, Geneva, Musée d'Art et d'Histoire, Ms. no. 1958/176-234. See the translation of this text in the present catalogue.

64. *Self-portrait*. (1917-1918). Oil on board.
16⅞ x 13″. Musée d'Art et d'Histoire, Geneva.

[15] Hodler, "The Mission of the Artist," Fribourg, 1897. See the translation of this text in the present catalogue. [16] I am indebted to Marilyn Kaye Hodson for some of the research on the relationship of Hodler to modern dance, which she carried out in a research paper at the University of California, Berkeley, in 1971. [17] Stephanie Guerzoni, *Ferdinand Hodler*, Geneva, 1957. [18] Quoted from researched documentation provided by Jura Brüschweiler. [19] Peter Selz, in Selz and Constantine (eds.), *Art Nouveau*, The Museum of Modern Art, New York, 1959, p. 74. [20] Hodler, "The Mission of the Artist," Fribourg, 1897. See the translation of this text in the present catalogue. [21] Rainer Maria Rilke, "Herbst," from *Das Buch der Bilder*. Translation by the author. [22] Hodler, interview with Else Spiegel, in *Wiener Feuilletons- und Notizen-Correspondenz*, January 21, 1904. [23] "Uber Hodlers Tektonik," *Die Kunst in der Schweiz*, May, 1928, p. 97. [24] "Ferdinand Hodler wie ich ihn erlebt habe," *Die Ernte*, Basel, 1943. [25] Hodler quoted by Arnold Kübler, *Du*, August, 1953, p. 9. [26] Carl Gebart in *Frankfurter Zeitung*, August 3, 1910. [27] René Daumal, *Mount Analogue*, San Francisco, p. 28. [28] Johannes Widmer, *Von Hodlers Letztem Lebensjahr*, Zurich, 1919, pp. 8–9. [29] Hodler to C. A. Loosli, in C. A. Loosli, *Ferdinand Hodler* (4 vols.), Vol. I, Bern, 1921, p. 11. [30] *Ibid.*, p. 5. [31] *Ibid.*, p. 472. [32] Jura Brüschweiler, "Ferdinand Hodler: Le cycle de la mort d'Augustine Dupin (1909)," translated by Jane Nicholson, in Institut suisse pour l'étude de l'art, Jahresbericht und Jahrbuch, Zurich, 1966, p. 167. [33] Hodler in his notebooks, cf. C. A. Loosli, *Hodler*, Bern, 1924, IV, p. 223. [34] Hans Mühlestein and Georg Schmidt, *op. cit.*, pp. 484, 487–488. [35] See below, pp. 90–100. [36] Johannes Brahms in Fritz Widmann, *Erinnerungen an Ferdinand Hodler*, Zurich, 1918, p. 6.

Ferdinand Hodler: Draftsman

Phyllis Hattis
Visiting Curator, California Palace of the Legion of Honor
and M. H. de Young Memorial Museum, San Francisco

Hodler's drawings, even more than his late landscape paintings, provide the essential evidence of his identity as a twentieth-century artist, specifically a twentieth-century draftsman. This is manifest in his preoccupation with line as a structural rather than strictly representational element, in his use of contour to define distance between parts and to mold the pictorial space around it. Hodler's line creates three-dimensional forms; it does not stand autonomously as a decorative element on a flat surface. His line may create patterns, as in his drawings around 1900, which reflect the Art Nouveau tastes of his period. Yet this line continues both to delineate figural forms three-dimensionally and to bind the compositional elements into an overall structural entity. A drawing by Matisse or Picasso of about 1906 seems more rooted in nineteenth-century values of line as a means to represent images than do Hodler's drawings during that same period. Hodler's drawing style of 1907 is closer to the style of Picasso or Matisse in the 1930s and 1940s, and always closer to the structural character of the drawings of Cézanne than to the linear configurations of Degas.

Whether primary or secondary aesthetically, cosmopolitan or provincial historically, Hodler's drawings and paintings attest the artist's awareness of both the art of his time and that of the past. Through his education with Barthélemy Menn and his subsequent travel, Hodler was exposed to major figure and landscape painting in France and Germany, especially during the second half of the nineteenth century. He had access to reproductions in the myriad art periodicals from the 1880s on[1] The impact of these publications may be seen by comparing Hodler's sheet of studies of a reclining couple for *Love* (1908) with Puvis de Chavannes' for *Le Sommeil*, reproduced in *Gazette des Beaux-Arts*, XXXVII (1888), 2ᵉ per., pl. 6. For figure painting he looked to France. His early work recalls Courbet, Corot, then Cézanne. Degas was a strong influence on Hodler in the 1880s and 1890s; the two men had dined together in Paris in 1891. Puvis de Chavannes, a champion of the young Hodler, steered the artist into exhibitions in Paris where his work was juxtaposed with Rodin's. His late landscapes reflect Monet (Hodler's last *Shore of Lake Geneva*, 1918, vs. Monet's *Charing Cross Bridge*, ca. 1900). Through Hodler, the artist who shared and extended the artistic ideals and objectives of his contemporaries, the period style from 1890-1918 in European painting becomes clearer.

The drawings of a strong draftsman often tell more of the artistic concerns of the painter or sculptor than do his monumental works. Hodler may be linked with Matisse, Picasso, Rodin, Degas, and Ingres in his strength of draftsmanship and in the amount of information contained within each drawing, whether quick sketch or finished composition. A serious draftsman, Hodler drew incessantly; he painted on canvas and drew on paper almost simultaneously, as well as drawing with pastel or graphite over the painted canvas itself. His hand recorded what his eye absorbed, sketching from nature or simply from memory[?] Hodler solved visual problems through a multistaged

Study for "Love." (1907–1908). Graphite and
white gouache on paper. 12⅞ x 14¾". Collection
Kurt Meissner, Zurich. [Not in exhibition.]

Puvis de Chavannes (France, 1824–1898). *Study
for "Le Sommeil."* [Not in exhibition.]

The Shore of Lake Geneva. (ca. 1918). Oil on canvas. Musée d'Art et d'Histoire, Geneva. [Not in exhibition.]

Claude Monet (France, 1840–1926). *Charing Cross Bridge.* (ca. 1900). Oil on canvas. 23⅝ x 39⅜". Musée Marmottan, Estate of Michel Monet. [Not in exhibition.]

process directed toward a highly structural, final painting, sometimes repeated several times. More than nine thousand drawings are preserved in Swiss museums and private collections, not to mention the cache in the Musée d'Art et d'Histoire in Geneva which contains 230 albums with over 12,000 sketches.[3] Yet it does not require evidence of this quantity to discover that Hodler's draftsmanship reveals a hand constantly in action, recording a chain of thoughts throughout the day, conveying private as well as easily read guidelines which function in his art. His range of draftsmanship spans the quick, thumb-nail sketches (nos. 100, 116-117, 118-a-c), the careful, detailed drawing of a compositional study (no. 87 or 94), the highly schematized and purified rendering of line (nos. 101, 103), as well as the unguarded utterances of his heart (nos. 106-114). Hodler drew for himself, to define and resolve his own artistic objectives. A few drawings were sold. A few more were given away. Some, since they were coveted, were marked, "p/a/v" meaning pas à vendre, indicating a noncommercial restriction attached to the work from the time of its making (nos. 107, 109, 110, 112).

Hodler thought and painted in terms of drawing, progressing from line, to form, to detail of figure and background. Line was his protagonist, the means of representing an idea, not merely the means of covering a surface. A working drawing might precede a painting and include the essential pictorial problems of concern at the moment, while another of a similar subject might succeed the finished painting by hours or years, serving as a catalyst for a variation on a familiar theme. His drawing contains fluid ideas, yielding changes until the last stroke of a pencil touched the sheet of paper or the brush a canvas, generating many canvases over the course of years. *Day*, 1898, thus develops into *Truth*, 1902, and further into *Floraison*, 1911–1913, and *Blick*, 1916, while *Night*, 1890, is transformed by 1908 into *Love*.

Hodler's dependence on drawings influenced the proportional relationship between his design and his scale. As an artist of his time, Hodler measured his success as a painter by his mural-size works. This academic standard of evaluation still prevailed in the late nineteenth and early twentieth century. But, in fact, Hodler's best work is in small scale, where the underlying structure of drawing in his painting strengthens and harmonizes with the painted brushwork. When restrained to the easel, Hodler preserves the scale of the original conception modified and controlled, as it is developed in the process of drawing. Blown up to wall-size dimensions, the design and the pictorial idea seem out of proportion to the means of rendering.

To study the draftsmanship of an artist first requires determining the interdependence of style and technique in his drawing. Analyzing the interaction of these two elements, in the category of drawing in particular, enables one to trace the development of a twentieth-century painter more effectively and more directly than surveying only the paintings of that artist. Hodler

96. *Study for "Love".* (1908). Graphite on
  paper. 9⅛ x 14½". Collection Bruno
  Giacometti, Zurich.

is a case in point. His experimentation with technique is far-reaching. His drawings convey the artist's serious concern with how a given medium, whether graphite, pen and ink, water-color, oil, or wash, is both applied and controlled by chosen tool, pointed or blunt, broad or narrow, rigid or flexible, as it makes contact with a paper support, resistant or absorbent to the medium and means of application. Hodler plays with the ways technique can alter both the conception itself and his skill in articulating it.[1]

While each technique became associated with a method of drawing and working, each method in turn generated a stage of pictorial development in the course of making a painting. In general, Hodler initiated the idea and developed a pictorial concept by what seems to have been almost continuous draw-ing. Literally hundreds of drawings, representing detailed step-by-step changes, exist for major figure compositions. Examples of working sheets expressing detailed changes following in sequence on separate sheets or on a single sheet are nos. 96-98 for *Love*, and no. 99 for *Sacred Hour*. Particularly after 1900, when Hodler's working habits were well established, his draw-ings for large-scale figure paintings are generally rendered on fine quality white wove Fabriano paper with a rough tooth texture. To complement this textured paper, Hodler drew with a medium-soft graphite lead as well as a rather broad-pointed pen inked with black. Sometimes he drew on a smooth-textured brown wrapping paper, perhaps on a roll, used in the same way as the Fabriano paper to sketch from nature, or else on a small pocket-size notebook sheet with a printed squared grid.

An artist embodying the pictorial concerns of his time, Hodler, like Rodin,[2] invented a method of drawing to express a philo-sophical and aesthetic point of view.[3] Hodler said that an artist must identify, order, and control the visible, that which is seen before him. The artist thought his eye must guide his hand, not permitting a conscious mental approach to predominate. For Hodler, a faith in the veracity of seeing, of recording, and being capable of graphically articulating what is seen is finally paramount to any idea whose source resides in imagination. A symbolic meaning is only authentic if it is an outgrowth of the basic visible substance, the evidence. Hodler combined the visible and symbolic raw material of his mature style in a theory he termed "Parallelism," a system rooted in seeing patterns in nature that parallel each other, for example, forms and their reflections, forms in pairs, repeated shapes, intervening spaces between forms and converse images of those forms. The pattern formed by repeated lines and reflected shapes was Hodler's means of ordering raw visual data. The working method he evolved from theoretical perception employed the monotype. Hodler began with a pane of glass, a square of at least twelve inches, through which he viewed his subject, a model or land-scape view, at the distance necessary to be enframed by that glass. With his brush loaded with gouache or oil paint,[4] he would begin by painting on the glass, tracing the outlines of the

97. *Study for "Love"*. (1907-1908). Graphite on paper. 8½ x 14⅝". Collection Kurt Meissner, Zurich.

98. *Lovers*. (1907-1908). Graphite on paper. 5⅛ x 10¼". University Art Museum, Berkeley.

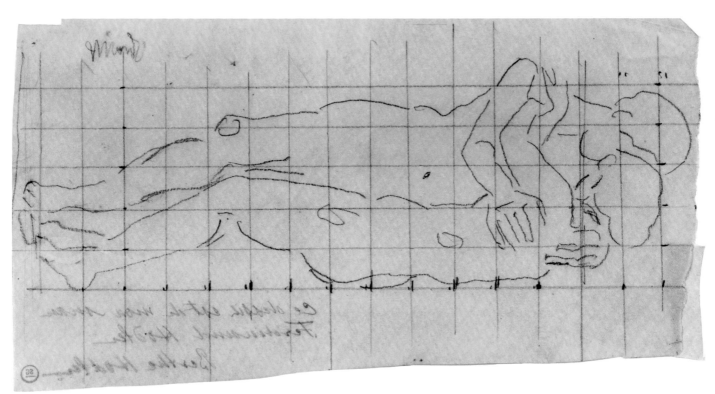

subject which it framed. With the general contours and some interior details of his subject recorded with a brush line, he then usually transferred the image to Fabriano paper, thus using the pane of glass as a printing plate to make a reverse image. When the print or monotype was sufficiently dry, Hodler traced on its reverse side with a medium-soft graphite point, probably by placing the sheet of paper against a lighted window. The drawing in graphite became the recto of the sheet, the monotype the verso. The recto image now approximated the pose that Hodler had originally viewed through his glass. An example of this drawing method is no. 92, a figure study for a large multi-figure composition for the University of Jena, painted during 1907–1908. The graphite image on the recto of the sheet is more than just a reverse of the original glass print; it is a simplification of it, more tightly structured in form. Contours are controlled to reflect each other, abstractly symmetrical. Interior details of form and clothing are added, sometimes stylized to create repeated lines and implied open shapes. Hodler claimed that this method of working was simple. But indeed, it was rather complicated and required time, not only to wait for the paint to dry before tracing, but also to move from one stage to another. Granted, it enabled him to integrate the processes of drawing and painting. But Hodler must have found other reasons for employing this method repeatedly, reasons more justifiable within the theoretical context of Parallelism than as a formal necessity in his pictorial enterprise. Indeed, when he released himself from the curb of this systematic bias and drew without the apparatus of monotype or Dürer's grid-proportions technique, Hodler's drawings reached unprecedented heights of beauty and strength. Witness the studies of Valentine Godé-Darel (nos. 100–102, 106–114) that rank among the finest drawings of this century.

Hodler used the glass print to see paired, reversed images, parallel and in opposition.[8] He must have believed that by tracing, translating exactly what he saw before him, he could achieve the greatest degree of accuracy in an oil or graphite rendering. His imagination was contained by the glass pane in the monotype stage, only to be freed to design in the second stage, in the graphite tracing of that image. He must have rationalized his convoluted working method as Rodin probably did in his procedure of continuous drawing.

Many of Hodler's drawings in graphite are rendered within a squared grid. Sometimes these drawings form the recto of a monotype image, sometimes not. They represent another method of working which could be sequential to the pictorial development of an idea first transferred from glass by monotype (as in many figure studies for *Glance into Infinity*) or simply an alternative method to monotype, achieving many of the same goals of accurate translation to a two-dimensional surface. The group of grid-contained drawings are derived from a method published by Dürer to draw a standard proportioned human figure according to his prescribed tenets. In the Hodler archives of the Kunsthaus, Zurich (Hodler archives no. 118),

92. *Figure Study for "The Departure of the Volunteers in 1813".* (1907-1908). Recto: graphite on paper. 22½x17½". Kunsthaus Zurich.

92. *Figure Study for "The Departure of the Volunteers in 1813".* (1907-1908). Verso: oil on paper. 22½x17½". Kunsthaus Zurich.

Study of Male Figure Proportions. 1875. Graphite on paper. Kunsthaus Zurich, Hodler Archives 118. [Not in exhibition.]

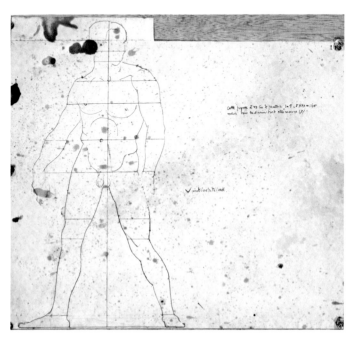

Mr. Brüschweiler has found a set of drawings by Hodler, taken from Dürer's publication, *Les Quatre livres des proportions humains* (Paris, 1557). This French publication was available to Hodler in Geneva in 1875. The grid was pre-drawn[9] and the figure then delineated in predetermined proportions according to its scale (cf. nos. 96–98). The process fundamentally reverses the technique of transferring and enlarging an image, by means of a superimposed grid. In such a technique the artist moves from the small scale to a scale that approximates life. Guided by Dürer, the artist transposes the life-size scale of an actual model, into a greatly reduced image drawn on a previously imposed, arbitrary grid.

In addition to Hodler's highly systematized drawings, either of the monotype or the proportioned group, there exists a third set conveying a more relaxed, spontaneous drawing style, a series of small-scale drawings rendered from memory or at least freely guided by imagination.[10] Nos. 116–117 consist of sets of compositional ideas, rendered in pen and ink, sometimes with graphite underdrawing, on sheets of graph paper (whose average dimensions are 5⅜ x 8½″). These drawings are initial graphic conceptions for eventual easel and mural-size paintings. As mere small notations, they provide evidence of the origins of scale for Hodler's large painted works, and illustrate the disparity between conception and execution often observed in the final work. These small studies contain major clues to Hodler's evolving graphic thought process. As if a reflection of man's own organic growth, Hodler's first idea (no. 117a) emerges from an ovoid compositional structure, containing tiers of figures reflecting each other as they bend and sway in perpetual motion, as if still in a state of prenatal evolution.[11] In no. 117b verso, the original fluid, ovoid conception is structured into two distinct tiers of figures, implying a shallow, horizontal compositional format. The figures maintain their original character in their reflecting postures and contour lines, now however developed into male and female beings. In nos. 117b recto to 117f the artist is guided more by the mobile living model than by the mind's eye (no. 117e);[12] breaking down the relatively static two-tiered composition of 117b verso. His pen traces a path of lateral arching movements of human form in a tangible earthly space, separating ground from water or sky. Parallelism reigns in the paired figures (no. 117d) or in the isocephalic arrangement (no. 117c). The studies for *The Battle of Morat* (no. 116a-c) repeat these progressive stages of conceptual and pictorial evolution as Hodler's initial idea develops into a structured, bileveled figural composition.

117a. *Preliminary Sketch for "Floraison"*.
(1916-1918). Pen and ink on paper.
3¼ x 8⅛". Kunsthaus Zurich.

117b. *Preliminary Sketch for "Floraison"*.
(1916-1918). Pen and ink on paper.
4¾ x 7⅞". Kunsthaus Zurich.

117d. *Preliminary Sketch for "Floraison"*.
(1916–1918). Pen and ink on paper.
4⅝ x 7⅞". Kunsthaus Zurich.

117e. *Preliminary Sketch for "Floraison"*.
(1916-1918). Pen and ink on paper.
4⅞ x 8¼". Kunsthaus Zurich.

Eventually Hodler arrived at a stage of pictorial development that incorporated yet another working method, collage, which he employed to structure further a maturely developed compositional idea. An indirect outgrowth of no. 117b recto is a collage for the same composition (no. 104). Its now fully developed figures are cut out and positioned in a flowing linear path against a brown sheet of paper that silhouettes their forms. Collectively, the gestures of the figures map the movements of a single form in space, here captured at different moments in time, analogous to, say, a set of 35mm film frames. In Hodler's collages, it is possible to distinguish his style and intention of rendering a figure moving through space from that of his contemporary, Rodin (*Cut-out Figures*, ca. 1900–1906).[13] For Hodler the energy is contained in the densely filled, shallow, almost electrostatic field around the figures. On a two-dimensional surface, Hodler documents the individual moments in the course of a movement; Rodin, the sculptor, embodies in one gesture of one figure all the movements that precede and succeed the moment of a movement.

Hodler's working methods and associated techniques continued to develop during the course of his career. As his drawing style matured, his concepts and methods of work and his preference of tools to express his pictorial tenets became standardized. Conversely, as his competence in handling certain techniques of drawing increased and a sequence of work proved effective in his manner of painting major-scale canvases, his style evolved. It crystallized into a fundamentally structural ordering of form and color whose line is relatively uniform and subservient to the overall structural necessities of the composition.

104. *The Great Joys of Life (Floraison)*. (ca. 1911-1913). Collage, graphite, ink, and gouache on paper. 29½ x 39⅜″. Collection Rudolf-Emil Schindler, Ligerz.

Auguste Rodin (France, 1840–1917). *Cut-out Figures.* (ca. 1900–1906). Paper collage. 22½ x 28½″. Princeton University Library, Princeton, New Jersey. [Not in exhibition.]

Unlike Picasso or Ingres, Hodler's style developed in one direction rather than many. His style is discernible in the two earliest works in the exhibition, nos. 68 and 69. The landscape scene, (no. 68) from ca. 1870, painted for sale to tourists,[14] executed before Hodler received any substantial training, illustrates the young artist's penchant for containing a rather flat, open foreground shape within an illusionistic background scene. This bold compositional arrangement is balanced by the horizontal and vertical lines of force on the periphery of the composition rather than in a classical mode, along the central axis of the composition. It complements the slightly later study of a bull (no. 69) from 1878–1879. This figure drawing contains the style of Hodler, tempered by rigorous academic study in the tools of draftsmanship and painting taught him in Geneva by Menn. Menn, as a late student of Ingres in Rome, 1838–1840, must have guided Hodler's ability to capture the basic form, mass, and contours of this bull. Hodler does not adopt Ingres' continuous contour line that creates simultaneously a three-dimensional form as well as a two-dimensional pattern. The emphatic pen line, sometimes following and sometimes diverging from the graphite underdrawing, is almost brutal in its metallic strength. The line, though it creates cubistic volumes through internal cross-hatching, is not essentially a contour line moving around a figure. Instead, the line is rather uniform in character, one that short-circuits and defines the structure of the form by its interior markings. Hodler's bull drawing extends to the figure the compositional style of his earlier mountainscape, constructing a relatively flat foreground space into a harmony with the background illusionistic space.

Early architectural studies of interior and exterior scenes further reflect the artist's structural character of style, in figure as well as in spatial rendering. No. 70, a small pen and ink sketch of a Spanish street scene from 1878–1879, illustrates Hodler's ability to render a living scene, sketched from nature, with all the sense of a direct, spontaneous reaction to it, but contained within a tight, architectonic composition. From his vantage point on the balcony in the left foreground, Hodler drew the life of that particular street as well as the view he had of it, composed according to a system of one-point perspective, a space at once narrowing and widening as it recedes. No. 71, an interior scene of a bar (typically Spanish) of ca. 1879,[15] shows Hodler's skills in rendering with graphite a composition balanced more by tonal harmonies than by perpendicular lines of force. Despite the potential vagueness built into a tonal construction (versus a linear one), Hodler's interior scene is felt in all its solid, cubic character. Young Hodler may be identified with Degas in employing a technique known as "contre-jour." The interior scene is illuminated by a light source from the rear, which silhouettes the objects in front of it. Degas used this technique in his portraits of the early 1870s.[16]

68. *Lake Brienz.* (ca. 1870). Brush and water-
    color on paper. 5⅛ x 8¼″. Collection
    Rudolf-Emil Schindler, Ligerz.

70. *A Street of Madrid.* (1878-1879). Ink on
    paper. 7¼ x 4¼″. Kunsthaus Zurich.

69. *Bull.* (1878-1879). Pen and ink on paper.
    5⅛ x 6″. Kunsthaus Zurich.

71. *Spanish Bar.* (1878-1879). Graphite on
    paper. 5¼ x 8⅛″. Kunsthaus Zurich.

Hodler combines the tonal, architectonic style of rendering seen in no. 71, in a figural composition, no. 74, a work from ca. 1888. A mother and child are rendered as fully massed, rounded volumes, toned with stumping, and contoured with line. These are representative of Hodler's early figure style, as are nos. 72 and 73.

The tempered contours, the rounded continuous silhouette, and the full volumes used to define the human form were radically altered by 1891 (no. 76). The transformation from rendering the figure with relatively smooth and curvilinear contours, to employing an open contour, brittle yet delicate, a line expressive of a distinct emotional or spiritual state, probably occurred in 1890 while Hodler was working on *Night* (see discussion by Peter Selz on page 30). Ironically, only a few drawings remain for this painting to enable the art historian to trace the change of style. However, for the work which stands as a quasi-pendant for *Night*, called *Day*, painted roughly eight years later, a range of drawings exists to document the figure development and styles of rendering that precede the

74. *Mother with Child.* (ca. 1888). Graphite
on paper. 12½ x 19¼''. Kunsthaus Zurich.

76. *The Disillusioned.* (1891-1892). Graphite
and crayon on paper. 11⅞ x 6''. Collection
Kurt Meissner, Zurich.

final version. The first sketches represented in no. 82, are generically in the style of the early compositional ink sketches (nos. 116–117), here developed with a variety of media (graphite under watercolor, with pen and ink). Horizontally composed in a space depicting the shore of a lake, the figures seem to be rising from a crouching embryonic position and revolving back to it, moving from left to right sequentially. The contours of these male forms are open and of modified curve. With the same androgynous figure type[17] Hodler shifts the sex from male to female, the lines of contour becoming more uniform, in a subsequent compositional idea (no. 83). As the idea of diurnal light, embodied in a female figure, moves laterally across a widely arching horizon, Hodler marks each movement with a specific gesture.

Specific studies (nos. 84–86) show figures rendered in fully realized volumes formed by rectilinear shapes of cross-hatched lines (no. 84). The line is full of movement and change of balance, tentative and undetermined. No. 85 depicts a figure bent too far over, who finally rolls over on her right side. Eventually, with a minimal amount of drawing, the line expresses pose, gesture, and mood, as well as anatomy of form. Volume is attained with minimal cross-hatching. Instead, a jagged contour, emphasized by repetition, contrasts with the interior zig-zag and C-curved strokes (no. 86). A developed compositional study (no. 87) which approximates the final painted composition, employs four media (graphite under watercolor, gouache, and finally overdrawn with pen and ink.) It combines these media with partial collage treatment (figures 1, 4 and 5, from the left). Poses still will be altered in the final painting, but their forms, gestures, and movements, defined by an emphatic black contour line (open in the drawing, closed in the painting), are now fixed. Modeling serves more as a reflection of daylight than as necessary anatomical articulation since the structure is well defined by the all-expressive and self-containing outer contours. Hodler, in his final painting for *Day*, as well as in the graphite figure study, no. 86, uses an outer contour line that silhouettes the figure as well as open contours that define its interior volumes, dissociated from the form it molds and the tangential spaces it welds. Inner form and outer spaces are inextricably joined by a highly schematized linear configuration that characterizes his paintings and drawings in the late 1890s. Hodler's line remains basically structural, not an aesthetic device, and cannot therefore be read as a pattern-making decorative element.

82. *Compositional Study for "Day I".* (ca. 1897). Graphite, watercolor, pen and ink on paper. 6⅞×20½". Kunstmuseum Bern.

83. *Compositional Study for "Day I".* (ca. 1898). Graphite and watercolor on paper. 7⅝×18⅞". Kunsthaus Zurich.

86. *Figure Study for "Day I".* (ca. 1898-1899). Graphite on paper. 8½×6⅝". Collection Kurt Meissner, Zurich.

The work of 1908–1918 reveals Hodler's later style: a simplified line creating a tighter compositional structure. His forms are more emphatically silhouetted, softened only by a graphite tool which produces a broad line that defines a plane (nos. 90, 91, 96–99, 101, 103, 105). The compositional ordering of parts becomes more homogeneous: the background becomes flatter, less illusionistic, and more consistent with the foreground. His figures become increasingly simplified. A coherent tapestry of pattern and color results, weaving in only a symbolic association with the natural world. For Hodler, the actual world is the space and furniture of his studio, and the lake and mountain landscapes nearby; thus, the combination of drapery and landscape elements in *Day* and *Love*. Shapes prevail over forms, color over light, plane over depth.

Outstanding in Hodler's total oeuvre is a set of drawings of his later period, which are linked by a common subject. They illustrate Hodler's strengths as a master draftsman. They also contain the fullest range of his handling of line, and his means of conveying a complete thought through a single line. These drawings are all of the woman he loved, Valentine Godé-Darel —either portraits, double portraits including himself, studies of her, or figure studies for which she is the model. These drawings began in 1909 and continued until her death in 1915. A graphite thumb-nail sketch of Valentine from 1909 (no. 100), expresses the excitement of a face mapped out by the artist for the first time, a face still somewhat unfamiliar. Previously disguised by a strong structural emphasis, Hodler's line is now almost featherlike and light (as in her hat strings). Cursory markings of form (in her cheeks and facial features) carry weight and energy unharnessed by the implied pressure or force of his drawing (in her hair).

100. *Valentine Godé-Darel Wearing a Hat.*
(1909). Graphite on paper. 6¼ x 4″. Collection Kurt Meissner, Zurich.

Double Portrait of Valentine and the Artist.
(ca. 1913). Graphite on paper. 10¾ x 8⅜″.
Kunsthaus Zurich, Hodler Archives. [Not in
exhibition.]

A profile portrait of Valentine (no. 101) is made by the mono-type method from about the same time, or just before. Its nearly pure silhouette is rendered with a soft broad graphite point. Its homogeneous line expresses a person as real and alive as she is depicted in the thumb-nail sketch (no. 100). Hodler's silhouette profile portrait recalls in technique and composition, more than in line, Manet's etched portrait of Eva Gonzales executed in 1870 but only posthumously published in the editions of Dumont (1894) and Strölin (1905). Manet's line connotes fluidity, and spontaneity. His consistent use of rather long curved contour lines is offset by short broad arcs that accent the predominant contours. Hodler's line is compara-tively terse, controlled in part by the tracing from the verso monotype image, and measured in its range of length and implied pace of execution. His line is never autonomous, never self-serving or memorable as a contour in itself. Remarkably, Hodler and Manet, who demonstrate contrasting use of line, both achieve a living likeness of a human being fully recog-nizable and present in its distinctive cursory presentation. Between 1909 and 1913, many drawings of Valentine are deper-sonalized studies, for which she models (no. 102). Her form is generally recognizable, yet the line of rendering is not peculiar to its subject.

101. *Valentine Godé-Darel in Silhouette.* (ca. 1909). Graphite on paper. 18⅞ x 13¼". Collection Rudolf-Emil Schindler, Ligerz.

102. *Figure Study for "Woman with Arms Spread Apart".* (ca. 1909). Graphite on paper. 14⅛ x 10". Collection Kurt Meissner, Zurich.

Edouard Manet (France, 1832–1883). *Eva Gonzales.* 1870. Etching. 9½ x 6¼". Achen-bach Foundation for Graphic Arts, Cali-fornia Palace of the Legion of Honor, San Francisco. [Not in exhibition.]

Late in 1913 Hodler learned that Valentine was fatally ill. Until her death in January, 1915, the artist drew and painted his beloved subject, as if by rendering her immortal on paper and canvas he could preserve her life. Seated beside her in the hospital room during the ensuing months, Hodler recorded her waning life, abstracting her pain, suffering, and agony in graphic terms, terms that must have protected him from madness. A profile portrait from late 1913 or early 1914 (no. 106) seems to portray the subject (and artist, by implication) during a moment of facing the irreversible truth. It is a stark contrast to the silhouetted profile portrait of Valentine five years earlier (no. 101). The head of Valentine is now rendered as if it were a rock, carved in chiseled planes out of a solid, earthly material, as three-dimensional and concrete as no. 101 is flat and elusive. With hard, straight line, Hodler adapts his personal style to a vocabulary of parallel lines that create planes, reinforced by coinciding as well as separately spaced, implacable line. The softness of a darkened line around Valentine's eye and mouth, as well as an occasional curved line in her hair or collar, is the only acknowledgment of her mutable state.

No. 107, a work of 1914, portrays Valentine seated in bed, with an expression that is at once questioning and imperative. Hodler is making both a portrait and a drawing. Never losing an intense eye-contact with Valentine, he represents her individual expression and character of form during this given moment. Yet, out of a dire need to objectify his image, Hodler turns the portrait into a design, an image of a full form, whose head is firm, contoured and toned with soft, stumped shadows. From this core, sweeping lines contour and fill the otherwise vast field of the paper support. In the area of hair and in the lower left bedsheet folds, Hodler electrifies his contour lines, using short C-curves, and aggravated multi-directional hooked lines in the bedding. Using a soft graphite, he proves how easily his line varies from curve, to plane, to an incised connotation.

106. *Valentine Godé-Darel (Profile to Right).*
     (1913). Graphite on paper. 12¼x9¼".
     Collection Rudolf-Emil Schindler, Ligerz.

107. *Valentine Godé-Darel, Ill.* (1914). Graphite
     on paper. 18½x20⅛". Musée d'Art et
     d'Histoire, Geneva.

Another work of 1914 (no. 108) reveals a greater deterioration in Valentine's state of health. Her bones protrude, her skin is taut. At the same time, a moment of joy and motion is conveyed in this depiction of Valentine and the child she and Holder shared, Pauline-Valentine, born the year before. Hodler's line acts as a rocker, lulling mother and daughter in peace. The focus is unequivocally on the mother, with her blurred contours.[18] The two are enveloped as one by the sweeping soft graphite lines that cushion them, providing a lyrical tone to an implied tragic, truncated episode. This lyrical line possesses a French quality of drawing rarely seen in his work.

Nos. 109–113 graph Valentine's decline and eventual death. On "Nov. 8, 1914," Hodler inscribes a work (no. 109) of that day to "Titine," his diminutive name for both Valentine and Pauline. Hodler's viewpoint is from a greater distance than usual. Composed at an oblique angle to the horizontal picture plane, the miniature form of Valentine is esconced in a set of curved and rectilinear planes. A distant horizontal line representing a floor plane grounds her bed that otherwise would be viewed as rising up the surface of the paper. This structuring of figure and object and interior space seen in no. 109 recalls the later drawings of Alberto Giacometti, a fellow Swiss artist and a generation younger.[19] Giacometti's drawing of *Chair and Floor*, 1953,[20] and Hodler's work no. 109 employ a graphite line that creates blurred contours. Line is transformed into plane, curved, straight, diverging, meandering. It defines the space of an interior rectangular cube as well as the figures and objects measured off within. Both artists possess a drawing style essentially structural in character, in this case consisting primarily of cubic planes that subdivide volumes and recompose them into graphite objects. Their compositions are preconditioned by the rectangle of the paper support or the inner frame drawn to reflect it (as in Giacometti), angled off or constructed in a frontal relationship to it. Both artists, as controlled draftsmen, use contrasting linear traits for counterbalance and accent. Thus a contour line that is long and curved is juxtaposed to a shorter stroke, faceted by brief intervals, forming an overall composition of tightly interlocking planes.[21]

108. *Valentine and Pauline*. 1914. Graphite on
    paper. 12¼ x 18½''. Kunstmuseum Bern
    (Bequest of Mme. Hector Hodler, 1964).

109. *Valentine Godé-Darel, in Bed*. 1914.
    Graphite on paper. 18½ x 24½''. Musée
    d'Art et d'Histoire, Geneva.

Alberto Giacometti (Switzerland, 1901–1966).
Chair and Floor. 1953. Graphite on paper.
19¾ x 12⅝''. Collection Herbert Lust, Chicago.
[Not in exhibition.]

In early January, 1915, Hodler drew Valentine asleep (nos. 110–111) as if preparing himself for her imminent departure. Her head propped against a pillow is set off as if it were an island in the middle of a fluid body (no. 110) or as a rock on a flat arid plain (no. 111). The contrasting modes of rendering create two entirely different moods of the artist toward his subject. No. 110 expresses a peacefulness through its swerving, gently curved lines moving up and down the energized field of space around Valentine's head. The flow of lines surrounding her head seems to unfurl from a tightly wrought wiry contour. By contrast, the angular, planar drawing of no. 111 builds up the form of Valentine's head through firmly drawn and measured parallel lines or overdrawn zig-zag markings that add texture to this stationary composition. The head, set off against a neutral field, prefigures Giacometti's analogous studies of heads (*Bust I*, of 1960, for example). No. 111 describes by implication the intense agony felt by the artist; the moment of agony portrayed is self-contained by the life nearly extinguished[22]

110. *Valentine Godé-Darel, Asleep.* 1915. Graphite on paper. 18½ x 12¼″. Kunsthaus Zurich.

111. *Valentine Godé-Darel, Asleep.* 1915. Graphite and gouache on paper. 13¼ x 19⅛″. Kunstmuseum Bern.

1915 F Hodler

1915 F Hodler

An Hans Mühlestein
F. H.

The head of Valentine continues to be the compositional anchor of the remaining drawings rendered by Hodler during the month of January, 1915. Symbolically and physiologically, her head becomes more substantial in its emotional reflections as her body diminishes in its weight and structure. By "19 Janv. 1915" (no. 112), her body is untraceable underneath the sheets. As the graphite line unwinds from her fully articulated head, it relaxes in its curves and stretches out its implied tension. By "24 Janv." (no. 113), Valentine's head is cachetic. The artist turns surgeon as his tool carves lines. On "26 Janv 1915" (no. 114), Hodler could only render a withdrawn image of Valentine Godé-Darel. Drawn in paint with graphite underdrawing, Hodler's line fills the vacuous white field of his canvas. Only the echo of Valentine remains. Her clasped hands and open-mouthed head are substantiated by a brushstroke of heavy impasto. Her surfaces are contoured and modeled with emphatic and assertive lines. He chooses murky, industrial tones for his palette that connote the unyielding quality of steel. Her bodily form and the spirit emanating from it, are contained in the dry brush lines, varied in shape, weight, and speed of rendering. The lines are analogous to human emotions, depicted by hooks, wiggles, and S, J, or U shaped marks. They crowd and hover over each other, intersect and interact, or contort in order to avoid involvement. Lines form shapes connoting spirits; the two pear-shaped forms with circular balls on top might even have been drawn unwittingly by the artist, to provide two guardian angels in vigil.

113. *Valentine Godé-Darel, near Death.* 1915.
Graphite and gouache on paper. 13½x
17⅞''. Kunsthaus Zurich.

114. *Valentine Godé-Darel, Dead.* 1915. Oil on
paper. 15½x25¼''. Oeffentliche Kunstsammlung Basel (Kupferstichkabinett).

Hodler recorded himself, forming a corpus of valuable paintings and drawings throughout his career that document his self-evaluation as artist and as man. A self-portrait (no. 115) made shortly after Valentine's death in 1915, dates from the artist's retreat and rest in Néris. Against a white gouache ground, so different from the flat white field of Valentine's last images, Hodler throws his own image out from the background, as if in low relief. The painted self-portrait, directly related to the drawn image, appears as a concave version. The image in the drawing conveys Hodler's shock in confronting his own vitality. The line is impelled with forward energy and a will to articulate a coherent and ordered form out of the chaos of his exhausted feelings. But his line lacks emotion. It is flat. Details are densely drawn with short strokes and self-contained contours, unevenly drawn, lacking in flow. The image, not the means, conveys emotion. The structural framework of Hodler's drawing has returned. Line draws and redraws over itself; gradually line serves plane, plane serves form, and form fits into a rectangular compositional format.

The graphic dialogue, composed of the studies of Valentine and Hodler's contemporary self-portraits during the years 1913–1915, uses a broad vocabulary and a poetic language unique in the oeuvre of Ferdinand Hodler. This set of drawings testifies to the vital and quintessential role subject matter played in the process of making an image during the early twentieth century. The style of Hodler and his generation was dependent on the emotional state of the artist as well as the symbolic content conveyed by his choice of subject. To objectify an image requires first intense subjective engagement. Through rendering the mutable as immutable, Hodler's personal life was at one with his art.

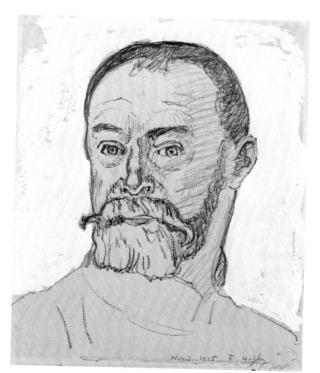

115. *Self-portrait.* 1915. Charcoal on paper.
15⅝ x 12¾″. Musée d'Art et d'Histoire,
Geneva.

Self-portrait. 1915. Oil on canvas. 15½ x 16¼″.
Musée d'Art et d'Histoire, Geneva. [Not in
exhibition.]

Notes

1 The publications, particularly art and design periodicals that expanded in number and scope at an unprecedented rate in the 1880s and 1890s, were accessible and doubtless invaluable as tools of learning for Hodler and his contemporaries. These periodicals focused on contemporary as well as past art. They were well illustrated with high-quality, full-scale reproductions, by means of printing processes well refined by the 1890s. For an excellent bibliography of the available periodicals listed according to country, particularly during the 1890s, see S. T. Madsen, *Sources of Art Nouveau*, Oslo, 1956. Madsen points out that between 1890 and 1900, one hundred periodicals on the applied arts alone were founded.

2 Hodler drew almost incessantly. His need to draw out an idea, to articulate a pictorial concern with pencil on a sheet of paper within reach, obviates the academic distinctions of classifying drawings as "drawings for paintings" or "autonomous drawings," just as it does such judgments as "finished" or "unfinished" drawings.

3 Mr. Jura Brüschweiler of Geneva is responsible for most of the major scholarly research and writing on Hodler's painted as well as graphic oeuvre accomplished during the past twenty years. His bibliography is vast and his standards of scholarship impeccable, as is his critical judgment. Mr. Brüschweiler has published a substantial segment of the drawings by Hodler in the following exhibition catalogues and museum publications: *Ferdinand Hodler Dessins*, Musée Rath, Geneva, 1963; *Catalogue des oeuvres de Ferdinand Hodler leguées au Musée d'Art et d'Histoire par M. et Mme. Hector Hodler-Ruch*, Geneva, n.s., XIII (1965); "Ferdinand Hodler und sein Sohn Hector," *Neujahrsblatt der Zurcher Kunstgesellschaft*, Zurich, 1966/1967. Mr Brüschweiler's cataloguing of the important public collections of Hodler drawings (in the Kunsthaus archives and drawings collection, Zurich, in the Kunstmuseum Bern, in the Musée d'Art et d'Histoire, Geneva, and in the Kunstmuseum Basel) develops and improves upon the scholarship of his precursor, C. A. Loosli, *Ferdinand Hodler, Leben, Werk und Nachlass*, vols. 1–4, Bern, 1921. I dedicate my essay on Hodler's draftsmanship to Mr. Brüschweiler, who has been so generous in guiding me through my exploration of that subject, and to Mr. Josef Müller, of Solothurn, whose collection of Hodler's paintings provided me with a legacy of the artist that is unique in its beauty and excellence.

4 Viewing a drawing in terms of the interrelationship between style and technique requires recreating the drawing itself. That is, in perceiving the work, the viewer attempts to reconstruct the *process* of making that drawing, tracing the development of a pictorial idea in time through the effects of the medium employed and technical materials supporting it. Then can one begin to understand the reason for choosing a given medium to create a specific kind of image. Then can one separate, to a degree, the properties of technique from the elemental quality of style.

5 Albert Elsen suggests in an essay on Rodin's draftsmanship that his technique of continuous drawing, often coupled with wash, evolved out of the artist's determined goal of accurately translating what is actually seen. His method, developed from the late 1890s, physically required that the artist's eyes remain fixed on his model, rarely dropping to the sheet he draws on, once the drawing has begun (A. Elsen, "Drawing and the True Rodin," *Artforum*, February 1972, p. 67).

6 Hodler rarely intellectualized his pictorial process of evolution. However, in "The Mission of the Artist," a public lecture in Fribourg recorded in 1897, Hodler talked about art and the artist in specifically graphic, occasionally metaphorical terms:

...the better our means of expression, the better we can *delineate* her image...The impressions he received from the outside leave on him more or less deep and lasting *traces*...To reproduce that tree, we must know the proportions of its parts in relation to the whole and their relative distribution…What does a trained eye see? It sees in one glance not only the object but its contours, the whole…the proportions, the way in which the figures stand out from other figures…drawing, whose whole role is to represent the configuration of objects. To reproduce form, the draftsman disposes of lines and flat surfaces. Line by itself expresses the infinite…to express the logic of movement, and secondly to enhance the beauty, the character of the contour. Line can express all this…How do we see objects?…It is again through their *outline* that bodies stand out clearly from each other…[emphasis added].

[7] The hue, whether yellow, red or brown, does not seem to affect his image or relate to his subject matter. More likely, Hodler used a color that was readily available on his palette for a nearby painting. Hodler's monotype suggests that when picture-making he drew and painted on the same paper (often drawings without the monotype verso have smudges of paint on them, again reflecting a proximity to painting).

[8] Hodler's composition, a mural-size painting of *The Battle of Morat*, from 1915–1917, is centered around a foreground figure, rendered twice, in mirror image, inspired no doubt by the recto-verso of a monotype drawing for this work. [9] Occasionally the grid is drawn over the figures, suggesting that in such cases Hodler thought to check his proportions, rather than to transfer his image onto a larger canvas, since the image is not necessarily developed or closer to its painted form than in drawings rendered over the graphite-drawn grid. [10] According to one woman whom Hodler used as his model from about 1912 onwards, the artist always drew from the model, who posed in front of him, in a held position rather than in continuous movement. The gesture drawn was a joint achievement, guided as much by the model's mode of expression and anatomical character as by the artist's conception. [11] The two amorphous forms reclining along the lower arc continue the oval movement around the outer edges of the composition. [12] The dance-like gesture often chosen by Hodler reflects the growing interest in modern dance during the period, as well as parallel methods and analogous expressions of other artists, including Rodin. [13] Reproduced in part, in A. Elsen and J. K. T. Varnedoe, *The Drawings of Rodin*, New York, 1971, p. 100, ill. 89. The exact assemblage of figures on this sheet is not necessarily by Rodin himself; but the cut-out figures are considered to be formed by the artist. I am grateful to Victoria Thorson, a contributor to this publication on Rodin, for the fruitful conversations we had on the relationship of Hodler and Rodin, as seen through their drawing. [14] Hodler's "Erinnerungslandschaften" were the antecedents of the modern tourist picture postcard, "les boîtes destinées aux étrangers." From 1868–1870 Hodler practiced this commercial art form under Ferdinand Sommer, a specialist in this art trade, in Thun. [15] Identified by Roderick Hall as a Spanish bar, the subject suggests that this work was drawn in Spain, and dates from 1878–1879. An alternative interpretation of this drawing is "Reading Room," dated 1880–1885 (see Jura Brüschweiler, *Neujahrsblatt der Zurcher Kunstgesellschaft*, 1966/1967, p. 85). [16] This is only one example of Hodler's experimenting with light effects ("peindre clair"). The pictorial premises, adopted by Hodler, stem from the Impressionist techniques practiced in France in the 1870s, though they reflect more of Degas than Monet. There is some evidence that Barthélemy Menn also practiced the technique of "contre-jour." [17] The androgynous form, as a figure type commonly used by artists in the decade preceding 1900 and shortly thereafter, is referred to by Robert Pincus-Witten in his unpublished doctoral dissertation (R. Pincus-Witten, *Joséphin Péladan and the Salons de la Rose†Croix*, Department of Art, University of Chicago, August 1, 1968). [18] "As bodies have a fairly smooth surface,

their outline is very clear. When an artist, for the sake of softness, blurs the outside contour, makes it fainter or rubs it out, he sacrifices the inside rounded modelling, which becomes softer and more graded, and especially when the lighting demands clarity, his work is not truthful. This unnecessary softening is highly obnoxious. It shows at the same time incorrect draftsmanship, lack of inspiration, banality of vision. Those who use it imagine that softening is embellishing. But if a marked outline has its beauties, so have gradations. To justify those blurred outlines, the artist must place his model in a special light, or in semi-darkness as Carrière does it for instance, or Titian." (Hodler, "Mission of the Artist," Fribourg, 1897). [19] Alberto, age thirteen at the time of Hodler's drawing, no doubt visited Hodler in his studio when accompanying his father, Giovanni, who was a close friend of Hodler and fellow leading painter in Switzerland during this period. Hodler's ties to the Giacomettis included being the godfather to Alberto's youngest brother, Bruno, born in 1908. Alberto's familiarity with Hodler's work need not be overestimated in terms of influence. Suffice it to say that the young Alberto may have harbored, subliminally, characteristics of Hodler's draftsmanship that became overt in his late career. [20] H. C. Lust, *Giacometti, The Complete Graphics; and 15 Drawings*, New York, 1970, drawing 4, p. 191. [21] Overlap between A. Giacometti and Hodler in their draftsmanship can be seen even more clearly in two mountain landscapes: Hodler's *Breithorn* (ill. p. 57), ca. 1911, Kunstmuseum Lucerne— a work in oil, though with the character of a drawing, rendered through line—compared with Giacometti's lithograph of 1957, *Mountain in Maloja* (Lust, *op. cit.*, pl. 28). The two works are alike in compositional format and ordering, in their silhouetted central form, and in their delineation of volume. [22] Inscribed by Hodler to Hans Mühlestein, Hodler acknowledges approval of his biographer-critic in giving him this intimate gift.

Ferdinand Hodler: Writer Introducing a Few Texts by the Artist

Jura Brüschweiler

"Eye-heart-reason." With those three words, Hodler implied that each of his paintings was the outcome of three equally necessary stages of composition: observation, feeling, and thought. First, Hodler observes the object—figure or landscape—with such a penetrating intensity that he gives it a striking, unforgettable life of its own, so that the picture becomes etched in your memory, and once you know, for instance, his *Lake Geneva from Chexbres*, you can only see the real landscape through the eyes of the painter. His vision replaces nature. Second, the feeling aroused by the discovery of a motif, which determines its selection, underlies its observation, and influences its intellectual working out, is with Hodler as powerful as his vision. When you look at the very moving series of works inspired by the illness, the agony and the death of Valentine Godé-Darel, and at the self-portraits and landscapes which followed, you can understand the basic sensitivity—always controlled, however, by a clear mind and a vigorous will—that imbues all Hodler's vision. Finally, thought—the last stage of creation—has a most important role in his work; it includes the idea expressed by the painting as well as the technique needed to render it; in the end, it modifies and determines even his vision and his feelings.

Within each of Hodler's pictures lies a symbol. *The Student* of 1874, a self-portrait of the young painter, embodies his pledge to art. *Night* of 1890 represents, to quote his own words, "the great symbol of Death." *Dawn* of 1918 appears as a forecast of his own death, through the way in which he relates the horizontal character of the landscape to that of a dead body. Each of his large compositions, which he considered to be his major works, illustrates one idea and illustrates it doubly: through what is represented, and through the way in which it is represented. For instance, *Eurythmy* of 1895 symbolizes "Humanity marching toward Death" (Hodler), with five old men walking along a road scattered with dead leaves; by using several figures, the artist emphasizes the collective nature of their fate and stresses the feeling of its inevitability. The intrinsic link between content and form, the strengthening of an idea through the way it is represented, is a characteristic feature of Hodler's art.

I have tried to show the importance of the ideas underlying Hodler's works. To understand the letter as well as the spirit, to penetrate the significance of Hodler's symbolism, we must turn to the painter's writings as our first source. When all is said and done, nobody can talk about his painting better than the artist himself, and to gauge his talent it is as a rule useful to read his writings—if there are any, which is the case for Hodler.

Hodler, however, was in no way a writer. He had spent his youth in the German-speaking part of the Canton of Bern, and therefore his mother tongue was German; but he spent the rest of his life in French-speaking Geneva, and became practically bilingual. An orphan at fourteen, he had to earn his living and was mainly self-taught; his literary training, in particular, was limited to a course on French essay writing, which he attended at the age of twenty-two at Geneva High School. Doubly handicapped by his bilingualism and by scant schooling, he was not gifted for literary expression, unlike so many painters, from Delacroix to Klee, who were great prose stylists. Therefore, his intellectual personality may sometimes appear somewhat narrow and doctrinaire.

As we can see from the many writings on painting he has left[1] Hodler was strongly attracted by theory. This taste for systems had been fostered by his master Barthélemy Menn (Geneva 1815–1893), who had a gift for translating practical problems of painting into striking formulae, but it also fits the general trend of the last century toward a more intellectual approach to art. Between Impressionism and Dada—which emerged respectively at the beginning and the end of his career—Hodler, around 1890, invented Parallelism, at a time when Gauguin was creating "Cloisonnisme" and when Maurice Denis was developing his *Théories* on Symbolism[2] Unlike other aesthetic labels, Hodler's Parallelism is not an ambiguous name: it describes a principle of composition consisting of "the repetition of similar forms" (Hodler). However, beyond this formal definition, it rests on an ethical formulation which sums up the Swiss painter's *Weltanschauung:* "What unites men is stronger than what divides them." This democratic ideal makes Parallelism more than an aesthetic hobby-horse; whether we recognize its validity or not, it is the keystone of Hodler's whole work. It is also important to note that Hodler had already intuitively put into practice his Parallelism around 1885 in *Beech Forest,* for instance, long before he formulated it as a theory in his Fribourg lecture (1897). The vital part played by theory in Hodler's art and the interest of his writings on it is thus undeniable.

Those writings reveal, not a man of letters, but an artist fascinated by theory. They consist mainly of notes, rough drafts scribbled according to his preoccupations of the moment, in a style which can be awkward and rough, but is always concrete, sober and direct—going straight to the point, like his paintings. Hodler meant most of those remarks, casually tossed off on paper, for his own use; even those written for friends who were critics were obviously not intended for publication; we must remember that as we read them. In an initial approach, Hodler's writings throw more light on his work than anyone else's attempted analysis. That is why I have gathered in this catalogue a few examples, chosen among those which, although they are not literature, can be published and thus can help us to understand some aspects of this exhibition. For the American public, who will meet the painter for the first time, these texts will be a suitable introduction to his works, or at least to their mental germination. To English-speaking scholars we bring the first English translation of written sources—among which is the important essay on Parallelism—by one of the proponents of European *Jugendstil.* These documents will help in the comparison of Hodler's views on painting with those of his contemporaries—from Van Gogh to Munch, from Gauguin to Lautrec and Klimt—and will contribute, together with the exhibition itself, to a definition of Hodler's role in the aesthetic revival which occurred at the turn of the twentieth century. (Translated by Madeline Jay)

Notes

[1] Cf. in particular "Aus Hodlers schriftlichem Nachlass," in C. A. Loosli, *Ferdinand Hodler—Leben, Werk und Nachlass*, Bern, 1921–1924, Vol. IV, p. 179ff. Unfortunately, Loosli's publication of Hodler's manuscripts leaves much to be desired with regard to transcription and chronology. A large part of the correspondence as well as notes filling Hodler's notebooks are still unpublished, but are being edited. [2] Cf. Maurice Denis, *Théories (1890–1910), Du symbolisme et de Gauguin vers un nouvel ordre classique*, Paris, 1913.

Ferdinand Hodler (ca. 1880). [Photo by Jean
Lacroix, Geneva, courtesy Jura Brüschweiler,
Geneva, ©].

A Selection from the Writings of Ferdinand Hodler

Compiled and Edited by Jura Brüschweiler
Translated by Madeline Jay

The Painter's Decalogue (1874–1875)[1]

1. The measure of all visible things is the eye.
2. The painter must practice seeing nature as a flat surface.
3. He must divide, in a sensible, deliberate way, with all the mathematical accuracy he can muster, the part of the surface he wishes to render into geometric planes.
4. When he has thus divided his surface he will place in it the outline of the object he is reproducing, as concisely as possible.
5. The outline constitutes an expressive feature and an element of beauty in itself. It constitutes the foundation of all later work and therefore must be strong and accurate.
6. The more concise the outline, the stronger it will be.
7. The different surfaces resulting from the insertion of the outline will be treated in the same way as the original surface, that is to say, again divided into different parts until all mistakes in proportion have been eliminated and each part will be treated as a whole until the desired finish is attained.
8. The means of attaining accuracy are observation, comparison, and measuring.
9. To reach mastery of observation and comparison, the only way is a constant and untiring practice of the eye.
10. To establish accurate measurements, the human eye is not enough, and the artist should avail himself whenever he can of mathematical instruments such as compasses, yardstick, figure-square, plumb-line and ruler.

Notes

[1] The original of this text does not seem to have survived. One of Hodler's biographers, C. A. Loosli, claims that it was included in a notebook of the young painter, who could recite the *Decalogue* by heart forty years after composing it. Our English translation is based on the transcription of Loosli, who published the text twice with slight variations: once in *Ferdinand Hodler—Leben, Werk und Nachlass*, Bern, 1921, vol. I, p. 44 and 227f.; and a second time in *Aus der Werkstatt F. Hodlers*, Basel, 1938, p. 119f. Loosli dates the *Decalogue* from between 1875 and 1876; we believe it must be dated a little earlier, considering the obvious connection between this text and *The Student* of 1874 and *The Schoolboy* of 1875 (Oeffentliche Kunstsammlung Basel).

Physiognomy of Landscape (1885–1886?)[1]

The physiognomy of landscape in painting depends on the emotional elements of the landscape, that is, the impressions it awakens within us. That is a purely personal matter, although general impressions, common to all men, may emerge, in various degrees. A factor which contributes very much to making emotions more intense is their duration.

The landscape painter will take into account the various means which help to strengthen the emotional impact of his pictures.

Firstly, the size and format. The spectator must be able to embrace the whole range of the picture at one glance.

The draftsmanship must always be clear and outspoken, so that the essential structure of the landscape can be visible and impressive. Also, the composition must be striking so that it creates its impact at first sight. The essential emotion, the main accent, must be stressed so that no doubt is possible. The subdividing of a line or surface into extreme and mean ratio[2] can be very useful for the setting-off of the picture.

A painter must also understand thoroughly the light which bathes the landscape and choose the lighting most likely to render the most intense emotion. Light can give most important hints about the character and feeling of a landscape, as it can be bleak, harsh, intense, blurred, gentle, soft, dusky or sweet.

The coloring of a landscape depends on its lighting. Therefore, the painter must carefully distinguish between the different lightings of his picture.

The more memories or feelings the landscape awakens in us, the better it is, for it speaks directly to the eyes and heart. It is therefore important to focus the glance of the spectator and not allow it to wander.

If the painter wants his picture to be moving and striking, he will not use figures. The motionless character of the subject, compared to the presumed mobility of the figure must be taken into account, however relative it may be.

The landscape must have a character, express a passion or an emotion. Its character gives it individuality. The figures or anecdote not only add nothing, but weaken the deep and direct emotional impact.

The painter must have the will to be clear and the capacity of rendering frankly and without hesitation his own feelings. Only then will the painted landscape grip the spectator without fail and convey to him a deep and lasting impression.

Notes
[1] The manuscript of those notes of Hodler's on landscape has been lost. C. A. Loosli once lent me his copy of it, accompanied by the following lines: "Hodler wrote those remarks about 1885–1886 on two loose leaves which I returned to him because they also contained some personal records." This is not the place for a detailed discussion of Loosli's dating of this text; we can only regret that he did not document it, and add the following remarks: Hodler's notes on the *Physiognomy of Landscape* are still far from revealing a marked interest in "Parallelism"; there is no mention of symmetry, nor of the repeating of similar forms, nor of the effect of impressive unity it creates—all those ideas only emerge in 1896–1897 in the *Mission of the Artist* (cf. p. 119), but in 1885 Hodler had already painted the *Beech Forest*, a landscape in which Parallelism —although still in a spontaneous and not systematic form—is obvious. We would therefore tend to place this text before 1885. But, on the other hand, Hodler stresses here the advantage of banishing all figures and anecdotal interest from landscapes. But we still find figures in his own landscapes as late as 1892: it is only around 1894, after being subjected to some criticism on that account, that Hodler painted over the female figure walking on the road of his *Autumn Evening* of 1892. This could incite us to place the notes on the *Physiognomy of Landscape* around 1893. And so, paradoxically, this text could be dated either before 1885 or after 1892 if we rely on internal analysis and assume that there is a

relation between Hodler's theory and his practice in the matter of land-scape. Until definitive documents allow us to narrow down the dating of this text, we have to accept Loosli's dates—with a question mark. This is the first publication of this text. [2] This refers to the Golden Section, according to Euclidian geometry, that is, the asymmetrical division of a line so that the ratio between the smaller and the larger segment should be the same as that between the greater segment and the whole line. This "divine proportion" is one to .616 ("golden number").

Barthélemy Menn—Beginnings—Artistic Temperament (1891)[1]

Barthélemy Menn

I arrived in Geneva in 1873.[2]

I met Menn at the Musée Rath where I was copying Calame.[3] A bit of good advice from him impressed me. I wanted to avail myself of this man's encyclopedic knowledge.

A conventional way of painting had prevented me from seeing things as they are.[4] Menn made it his task to restore me to a state of nature and to make me capable of seeing. I remained for six years under his influence.

After two years, I painted *The Student (L'étudiant)*, *The Joiner (Le Menuisier*, 1875, Kunsthaus Zurich), *The Schoolboy (L'Ecolier*, 1875, Oeffentliche Kunstsammlung Basel)—which created a furor when they first came out in 1874.[5] The following year, in 1876, *The Gymnasts' Dinner (Le Banquet des Gymnastes)*, a cartoon to commemorate the centenary of the Beaux-Arts class, was very successful.[6]

(. . .)[7]

Beginnings

Daily struggles.

When I had nothing to eat for lunch, I would climb onto the roof of my workshop and play a tune on my guitar, which cheered me up.

As I went off to paint a landscape, I sometimes had just a dry roll for my breakfast and dipped it in a fountain on the way.

For years, I used to take off my cupboard door at night, to sleep on it.

In spite of it all, I was the happiest man in the world, I was free to come and go as I liked and under nobody's orders. Since I allowed myself the luxury of painting, I had to subordinate everything else to it and I gladly underwent all sorts of difficulties.

At that time I lived alone. I was unapproachable and shunned all society.

Things impressed me very deeply. The thing I see penetrates right into my vitals.

A reasoning imagination.

But, almost always, I see nature with a feeling of pain. I reproduce it because of that intense feeling.

Haunted.

Now I work out the effects after feeling them. I work them out particularly when I want to reproduce a feature of nature.

(. . .)[8]

The paintings *Tired of Living (Las de Vivre,* 1887, Kunstmuseum Winterthur) and *A Lost Soul (Une Ame en Peine,* 1888–1889, Oeffentliche Kunstsammlung Basel) sprang from painful times in my life, but generally I have a cheerful nature.

The critics, who have been too favorable to me, never had any influence on me. Anyway, they often contradict each other.

Notes

[1] Manuscript: Bibliothèque Publique et Universitaire, Geneva, Ms. fr. 2984/273–274. The manuscript has neither title nor date. Barthélemy Menn (Geneva, 1815–1893) was Hodler's master. Hodler wrote those notes for his friend Louis Duchosal, a poet and critic who used most of them in an article published in the *Tribune de Genève* on March 8th/ 9th, 1891 (cf. J. Brüschweiler, *Ferdinand Hodler—Anthologie critique,* Lausanne, 1970, p. 50ff.). This allows us to date the manuscript fairly accurately from February 1891. Hodler presents the various subjects mentioned in the following order: Beginnings—Artistic Temperament—Barthélemy Menn—Main Works painted from 1874 to 1890. To re-establish the chronological order of the facts narrated, we have allowed ourselves to place at the beginning the notes on Menn, who was Hodler's master from 1872 to 1878, and to follow with notes on his beginnings and his artistic temperament which in fact refer mainly to the years 1880–1890. Finally, we omitted the list of about ten works at the end of the text because most of them are not in our exhibition. The complete manuscript has been published in its original French version by Arnold Kohler, Bernard Gagnebin and André Duckert in the review *Club des Arts—Musées Suisses* No. 9, s. 1, May 1953, p. 6ff. [2] Various documents, among which a Certificate of Registration, allow us to state definitely that Hodler was already in Geneva in February 1872. [3] Hodler copied *Storm at Handeck (L'Orage à la Handeck,* 1872, Musée Sainte-Croix) by the Alpine painter Alexandre Calame (Vevey 1810—Menton 1864) whose naturalism with Romantic tendencies was opposed to the "plein-air," intimate painting of Barthélemy Menn, who was Corot's friend. [4] An allusion to the "Swiss Views" which Hodler had mass-produced in the workshop of Ferdinand Sommer at Thun. [5] In fact, it was in 1876, at the exhibition of the Société Suisse des Beaux-Arts in Geneva, that the works mentioned by Hodler created a sensation in the press (cf. Jura Brüschweiler, *Ferdinand Hodler—Anthologie critique,* Lausanne, 1970, p. 19ff.). [6] The cartoon of the *Gymnasts' Dinner* was destroyed by Hodler, but there is a version painted in 1877–1878 (Kunsthaus Zurich); both are reproduced in Jura Brüschweiler, *op. cit.* (note 5), p. 23. [7] Omitted part of the manuscript; a list of about ten works painted between Hodler's journey to Madrid (1878/1879) and *Night (La Nuit,* 1889–1890), mentioned without any comments. [8] Here in Hodler's manuscript was inserted the extract about Barthélemy Menn, which we placed at the beginning of this text, and the list of works which we omitted (cf. note 7).

My Present Tendencies—Night (1891)[1]

My Present Tendencies

I want to attain a powerful unity, a religious harmony. What I wish to express, to stress, is that which is the same for us all, what makes us alike; the resemblance between human beings.

Art has increasingly moved away from that conception since the Egyptian period. The Greeks, then the Romans, introduced more and more variety (variety within symmetry, with Michelangelo and Raphael). The present period is completely invaded by variety. Resemblances between human beings, large and simple harmonies are not translated. Technical preoccupations, small preoccupations are all that painters think about, instead of the whole. But art on a small scale is unreal.

I start from the great unity of life. There may be differences, but even more there are analogies.

This reform answers the need to express things on a larger scale.

I ignore accidental reality, small effects, witty traits, little sparks. The style of painting is subordinated to the form. I do away with whatever could distract the spectator from the whole.

The effect attained through color contributes to expression and completes it and makes things more visible. I consider color as an impressive element. It is a symbolist principle.

In the two paintings I am working on at the moment—*Tired of Living* and *The Saddened Souls*[2]—there is a uniformity in the gestures of the characters which expresses the same state of mind. The same tendency can be noticed in the coloring. *Harmony is achieved through similar chords.*[3]

Characteristics of my painting from the point of view of the visibility of the bodies represented:

(1) The outline of the figures stands out clearly. The outside character of the figure stands out as a whole. A whole group of figures is treated in that way.[4]

(2) The figures are clearly visible through their outline and take on an architectonic character: they are monuments of expressive architecture.

(3) The figures, the faces have striking physiognomic features.
(. . .)[5]

Night

Up to now, my most important painting, in which I reveal myself in a new light, is *Night*. Its appearance is dramatic. It is not one night, but a combination of night impressions. The ghost of death is there not to suggest that many men are surprised by death in the middle of the night, as the *Cologne Gazette* has claimed, but it is there as a most intense phenomenon of the night. The coloring is symbolic: these sleeping beings are draped in black; the lighting is similar to an evening effect after sunset, showing the approach of night, but the effect is completed by those black drapes which partially cover the figures everywhere; they are the low, muffled notes of an austere harmony, which is merely a transcription of the effects of night. But the most striking feature is the ghost of death and the way—both harmonious and sinister—in which this ghost is represented, hinting at the unknown, the invisible.[6]

Night is what I claim to be my first work; it is mine by its conception and setting. At the Champ-de-Mars[7] it was the most original picture.

My two paintings representing *The Saddened Souls* and *Tired of Living*[8] will, like the first, reveal the principles of an art which, if it is not exactly new, is at least more far-reaching and accessible to all.

P.S. The editor may agree or not with the town council[9]. I hope he will try to understand what I wanted to represent. My picture *Night* belongs to an order of ideas much above the intentions which were assigned to it. I considered *Night* as the great symbol of death and tried to render it by draped figures in attitudes which fit the subject.

Notes

[1] Manuscript: Geneva, Bibliothèque Publique et Universitaire, Ms. fr. 2984/361–366. The manuscript is not dated; the subtitle *Night* is our own addition. Hodler wrote these notes for his friend the art critic and poet Louis Duchosal. The information about the dating of this text is contradictory. On the one hand, some of the phrases used by Hodler in this text are also to be found in Duchosal's criticism of *Night* in the newspaper *La Revue* (Lausanne) of March 2, 1891 (cf. J. Brüschweiler, *Ferdinand Hodler—Anthologie critique*, Lausanne, 1970, p. 48); we could therefore deduce that Hodler's manuscript was written in February 1891. But on the other hand, the painter alludes to the favorable reception of *Night* at the Champ-de-Mars in Paris. If he means the reaction of the jury of the Salon of the Champ-de-Mars which accepted his picture in April 1891, the manuscript could date from that period and the occurrence of some of Hodler's phrases in Duchosal's article might either be a coincidence, or due to some other letter addressed by the painter to the critic. But if Hodler is alluding to the reception of *Night* during the exhibition at the Champ-de-Mars, which lasted from May 15 to July 10, 1891, the manuscript could date from about July 1891. Finally, Hodler mentioned as works in the making his *Disappointed Souls* and *Tired of Living*, both completed in 1892 (cf. note 2), but which he could have begun in March just as well as in July, 1891. In any case, the present manuscript can be placed, even if only approximately, during the first half of 1891. We have omitted here a passage describing half a dozen paintings earlier than *Night* because they are not included in our exhibition. The complete text has been published, with a few copying errors, by A. Kohler, B. Gagnebin, and A. Duckert (in: *Club des Arts—Musées Suisses*, No. 9, s. 1, May 1953, p. 8ff.), in the original French version. [2] *Tired of Living* (Munich, Neue Pinakothek und Staatsgalerie) is dated 1892 but—as this text proves—Hodler had already begun work on it in 1891. The *Saddened Souls*—later the *Saddened Geniuses*—are the first titles which Hodler gave to the composition which he finally called *The Disillusioned*, also dated 1892 (cf. no. 17). [3] Line crossed out by Hodler: "In that respect, *Night* is a translation." [4] Hodler had added, then crossed out: "Another point, already mentioned; my paintings strongly express my own character."

⁵ Omitted passage: a description of works earlier than *Night*. ⁶ Here Hodler added between brackets, for Duchosal's benefit: "You may quote the various articles which have been published." ⁷ This refers to the Salon du Champ-de-Mars in Paris, organized by the Société Nationale des Beaux-Arts, whose president was Puvis de Chavannes. ⁸ Cf. note 2 above. ⁹ The town council (Conseil Administratif) was, and still is, the executive power of the City of Geneva. Its President had demanded and obtained the banning of Hodler's *Night* from the municipal exhibition of 1891, although the jury had unanimously accepted it.

Interview: Ferdinand Hodler on his principles of art and on Klimt (1904)[1]

What I value most in painting is form. Everything else is there to serve form. Most important among these servants is color. I love clarity in a painting and this is why I love Parallelism. In many of my paintings I have chosen four or five figures in order to express this feeling because I know that impression is enhanced by the repetition of one and the same object. I prefer five figures because an odd number heightens the order of a picture and creates a natural center within which I am able to concentrate the expression of all five figures. If I were to select a larger number, the eye would not be able to encompass all figures simultaneously. I want to avoid this, so that unity and order will not be disturbed.

When I began painting, I turned toward Impressionism. But slowly, with many years of study and observation, I came into my current procedure: clear form, simple representation, repetition of motifs.

My favorite artists are Dürer[2] and the primitive Italians. Among the moderns, I value Klimt[3] very highly. I am specially fond of his murals: there everything is quiet and flowing, and he too likes to use repetition, which accounts for their splendid decorative effect. He also uses repetition frequently in order to emphasize a different grouping more clearly, almost like a background. For example, there is a painting in which stylized maidens stand close together in a meadow from which flowers are growing. Close by a man embraces a woman; the limbs of both figures are drawn next to each other in a parallel manner.[4] The thing which is so admirable in Klimt is the freedom with which he treats everything. He is a personality who goes entirely his own way. Yet at the same time his grace and tenderness are Viennese. Of the three ceiling decorations,[5] I know only *Philosophy*. This I like less than the murals and the portraits, but I can look at them not as a critic but as an artist, and Klimt's color harmony and pictorial manner of representation appear to me most admirable.

Klinger I like less; he always wants to say too much. Böcklin is very important, but a little too literary for my taste.

Notes
¹ Interview obtained by Else Spiegel and published in *Wiener Feuilletons und Notizen Correspondenz*, Vienna, January 21, 1904, at the time of Hodler's sojourn in Vienna. Gustav Klimt (1862–1918) was the principal

protagonist of *Jugendstil* in Vienna. [2] During his stay in Vienna in 1904, Hodler went to the Albertina each day in order to study the drawings and prints by Albrecht Dürer (cf. Adolf Frey, *Ferdinand Hodler*, Leipzig, 1922, p. 28). [3] Hodler met Gustav Klimt on the occasion of the exhibition of the Vienna Secession in January 1904. He even acquired a painting, *Judith*, by the Viennese painter (now in the collection of the Oesterreichische Galerie in Vienna). [4] Hodler speaks of the central group of Klimt's *Beethoven Frieze*. [5] In 1900 Klimt was commissioned to execute allegorical paintings of *Philosphy*, *Medicine*, and *Jurisprudence* for the University of Vienna. These paintings caused a great public controversy and were withdrawn by the artist. They were destroyed by fire during World War II.

Last Notes (1917–1918) [1]

Color exists simultaneously with form. Both elements are constantly associated but sometimes color strikes you more—a rose for instance—sometimes form—the human body.

What is different and what is similar

Uniformity as well as diversity exist within human beings. We are different from each other, but we are even more alike. What unites us is greater and stronger than what divides us.

When you look up at the sky, you have a feeling of unity which delights you and makes you giddy. The very expanse is striking.

When I am on the sea, I can only see the sky and water, a long line of infinite horizon.

When I look at the night, that is another instance of a large expanse.

When I see a dead man, the eternity of his silence moves me, impresses me deeply.

When I see similar forms, a certain order, I am also pleasantly affected. Why should a flower delight me? Because it consists of similar forms grouped around a center. Nothing delights us more than orderly forms.

For twenty years I have noted similar phenomena and reproduced those resemblances, those similarities.

There is also diversity—the different faces and characters of various people. And on the other hand, what is similar, analogous, general characteristics, the same feelings of humanity. There is a small truth and a larger Truth.

Art unites us. Long live art!

What makes us one is greater than what divides us.

I have expressed my likings: a rose, the sound of an organ.

Explanation of my Pictures

Night: A large expanse of a natural phenomenon, a large expanse of black shades.

Tired of Living: The sound of an organ.

Eurythmy: Five men representing humanity, marching toward death.

The Elect: A child surrounded by female figures. This picture is like a rose. What is a rose? Similar forms grouped around a center.

Unanimity: Union within the same feeling.

Glance into Infinity: Women, moved by boundlessness.

Notes

[1] Manuscript: Geneva, Musée d'Art et d'Histoire, notebook of F. Hodler, Inventory No. 1958/176–234. On the cover of this notebook appears the inscription "Last Notebook" in the hand of the painter's wife, Berthe Hodler. These "Last Notes" (the title is not Hodler's but our own) can therefore be dated from 1917 or even 1918. This is the first publication of this text.

The Mission of the Artist

A lecture given to the Société des Amis des Beaux-Arts in Fribourg, on March 12th, 1897[1]

The mission—if we can give it that name—of the artist is to express the eternal element of nature, beauty, to stress this essential beauty. He enhances nature by intensifying objects; he enhances the shape of the human body; he gives us a magnified, simplified nature, freed from all irrelevant details. He presents to us a work which is commensurate with his experience, his heart and his mind.

Art is a gesture made by Beauty. Plato gives this definition:— "Beauty is the splendor of Truth"[2]—which means that we must open our eyes and look at nature. Man can make nothing out of nothing; when the artist creates a work, he borrows elements from the existing world in which he lives. Even the richest imagination is guided, stimulated by nature, its greatest source of information. The deeper we penetrate into the spirit of nature, the more completely we can express her; the better our means of expression, the better we can delineate her image.

We reproduce what we love: this face rather than another; the delightful landscape we have enjoyed. Emotion is one of the first causes which impels a painter to create a work of art. He wants to convey the charm of a landscape, of a human being, of nature, which has moved him so deeply. The impressions he receives from the outside leave on him more or less deep and lasting traces, and the choice he makes determines the character of his work and his own character as a painter.

The eye.

Through our eye and our intelligence, we apprehend the beauties which surround us. As I said before, the image will be reflected more or less deeply according to individual perceptions and sensitivity. We are told that we must learn to see. An untrained eye does not see to the same degree as a trained one the shape and colors of objects; it does not grasp their character, the formal rhythm produced by movement, the attitudes and gestures of man. It does not observe the grouping of figures in everyday encounters. The untrained eye is also slower in noticing the movement of objects. But it recognizes somebody's face, while being completely ignorant of the exact shape of its features. It recognizes a tree, knows that it is a plane tree or some other species, that it is large or small—and that is about all, short of a detailed examination. To reproduce that tree, we must know the proportions of its parts in relation to the whole and their relative distribution. Above all, the untrained eye does not see nature in relief in relation to a flat surface. One must make a willful effort to see.

To train the eye, one must observe, compare forms to each other, examine attitudes, facial characteristics, one must look at colors and compare them. Our eye develops by looking at things. Obviously, it is the brain which sees and hears. But apart from that, the eye is an instrument which can be perfected, both in accuracy and aesthetic judgment. To see is to know an object in its proportions, such as they appear to the eye. Therefore, to see is to know. But although this way of seeing things from one point of view does not bring us to a true knowledge of real dimensions, nor even to the knowledge of the whole object, since we only look at it from one side, nonetheless we judge the whole appearance and its harmony. It is not enough to know what the object is really like, but also why it appears in that way to us; why does this vertical line seem vertical to me? Why does this tall man seem tall to me? As we said before, our eye is not such a precise instrument that it could reproduce, for instance, the portrait of an individual without previous training; otherwise everybody could draw portraits at the first attempt. Our eye, even when trained, cannot measure with precision; I might almost say—though nobody would like to exchange one for the other—that a pair of compasses is more accurate than an eye. We sometimes say— in French—that somebody has "a compass in his eye"—it is better to have it in one's hand, like Michelangelo, Albrecht Dürer, or Leonardo. However, all three must have had a better trained vision than ordinary mortals, since I have named masters who achieved through form a real power of expression.

What does a trained eye see? It sees in one glance not only the object but its contours, the whole; it grasps at once the proportions, the way in which the figures stand out from other figures, or in space it sees the effect of light. Often through his individual eye, a painter may see colors in a particular way, which adds a charm of its own; but if that was his only merit, his work would be second-rate. A genuine work of art must spring from the mind and the heart, that is superior vision.

Form.
A gifted man has an intuition of a harmony which he cannot yet define. He has opened his eyes to see the things he loves. Now he only needs an opportunity for this harmony to reveal itself in a way which only he has perceived. When the artist has an aim, when he is not content with reproducing a scene in an ordinary way, when he has a decorative purpose, he can concentrate on form, or color, or on effects of light and shade. In

nature, these three elements coexist, but one or the other is stressed. The artist who wants to concentrate on form makes color subordinate. While the artist who is more interested in color subordinates the form: Titian, Giorgione, for instance, and the most powerful colorists get their effects from color, while following the logic of things. They place a figure in the light or in the shade, not for the sake of form, but to obtain certain color effects, and they treat the whole composition with that intention.

No matter what the painter wants to attain, he cannot do it without form—a *sine qua non*. Nothing can be expressed without it, nothing is visible without it. We might say that it gives four-fifths of the likeness: the shape of bodies, space, the inward state of the soul—without any help from color. It is enough to examine all drawings, engravings, photographs, to be convinced of it. Moreover, form is common to all plastic arts: sculpture, architecture, painting. It is the most expressive element; it has, like color, a seductive charm. A straight line, a square, a circle, when we know their possibilities, can be impressive figures. We are also somewhat better equipped to represent form, for our means of expression correspond more exactly to the element we are reproducing. In painting, it is less disappointing than color. Form is the outward expression of a body, the expression of its surfaces.

From all this, we gather the importance of the drawing, whose role is to represent the configuration of objects. To reproduce form, the draftsman disposes of lines and flat surfaces. Line by itself expresses the infinite. The form of each object, as we perceive it, consists of an outside contour and inside forms. That is one of the results of our point of view, for in fact all surfaces of a body are outward. The contour not only expresses the width, height, and depth of a figure, it also has an orna-mental, architectural character by virtue of the fact that it stands out clearly from neighboring bodies; and also thanks to the intention of the artist—and that is the power of some great masters. The outline of the human body changes according to its movements and is in itself an element of beauty. There is almost always a conflict in this double search of the artist: first to express the logic of movements, and second to enhance the beauty, the character of the contour. Line can express all this. Nowadays, contour is given the more important part: it is stressed and therefore becomes ornamental. It can be said that applied art becomes more and more ornamental. But above all, great masters have in common this clear setting-off of the figure as a whole and looking for the linear beauty of a contour; they oppose long and short lines, stress the movement and the parts of the human body, express its rhythm.

How do we see objects? Through their standing out dark or light, through the contrast of light and shade, through the differences of color. It is again through their outline that bodies stand out clearly from each other, with the figure sometimes appearing light on a dark background, and sometimes dark on a light background. Because bodies have a fairly smooth surface, their outline is very clear. When an artist, for the sake of softness, blurs the outside contour, makes it fainter or rubs it out, he sacrifices the inside rounded modeling, which becomes softer and more graded, and especially when the lighting demands clarity, his work is not truthful. This unnecessary softening is highly obnoxious. It shows at the same time incorrect draftsmanship, lack of inspiration, banality of vision. Those who use it imagine that softening is embellishing. But if a marked outline has its beauties, so have gradations. To justify such blurred outlines, the artist must place his model in a special light, or in semi-darkness as Carrière does it for instance, or Titian. This toning-down has been used and abused because the public tends to like it. I was told by a photographer that ladies like softened and blurred portraits, and the more so the better. But I must add that it is not so much the outline they want subdued, as the modeling of the face. For my part, I know nothing more beautiful than some female portraits by Italian primitives, showing outlines of a remarkable clarity.

Color.
It characterizes and distinguishes objects, sets them off, and contributes very much to the decorative effect. Color has a penetrating, harmonious charm, independent of form. It influences emotions, causing joy, especially in the case of bright colors, which we associate with light, while dark colors engender melancholy, sadness, and even terror. White usually means purity, while black represents evil or suffering. A vibrant red expresses violence, a pale blue softness, purple sadness. The charm of colors increases according to their combinations; they harmonize or enhance each other like parallel ornaments; or they clash and produce contrasts.

The impact and influence of color is in proportion to its intensity, its extent, or its place amidst other colors which set it off or tone it down according to the propinquity of white or black. Combined with form, color stands out even more and stresses the rhythms created by variety and repetition; it is of course never separated from form, but form can strengthen its effect.

The coloring of objects changes according to the coloring of the light: nuances are different under a gray or a blue sky. Under a blue sky we are more cheerful, not only because of the clearness of the weather, of the contrast between lit and shaded surfaces, but also because of the pleasant interplay of the coloring of shadows, which instead of gray, are tinted with blue and purple, amidst which shine orange surfaces reflecting the rays of the sun. Under a fine blue sky, the shade is blue and purple, and under trees, ultramarine, and all the green leaves shine as a mass. What a pleasing sensation is produced by this harmony of green and blue! And the mountain brook, rushing toward the valley, seems sprinkled with large diamonds on a blue background. On the other hand, too strong a light tones down the beauty of reds and other colors, only transparencies keep their brightness, and flowers seem to suffer from an excess of light: their colors fade.

Color is also one of the great causes of disagreement between painters and the public. For a long time, people could not understand that a pink face could look purple outdoors, under a blue sky, and orange or even bright red, when lit up by the setting sun. The ordinary eye is not very observant, and above all untrained, and does not grasp the nuances which the artist reveals: they seem to the layman a horrible exaggeration.

The charm of colors is mainly in their blending, in the repetition of shades of the same color. Soft harmonies seem to penetrate you deeply, to go right to the heart. (I am thinking now of those harmonious lines in some fragments from the Parthenon friezes.) While contrasts excite and surprise you, seem to attack your nervous system, and the passing from a soft harmony to a contrasting effect is a frequent sensation in daily life. But all of these, the riots of color, the dark or pale spots, the contrasts, the varied harmonies of vibrant tones are an effect of the light: the universal charm of color and shade is derived from light.

The Work of Art.
If in my mind I compare the main characteristics of things which have made a strong and lasting impression on me, things whose ensemble has struck me most by its strong unity, I must acknowledge in every case the same element of beauty: parallelism. I shall now try to explain what I mean.

Parallelism, whether it is the main feature of the picture or whether it is used to set off an element of variety, always produces a feeling of unity. If I go for a walk in a forest of very high fir trees, I can see ahead of me, to the right and to the left, the innumerable columns formed by the tree trunks. I am surrounded by the same vertical line repeated an infinite number of times. Whether those tree trunks stand out clear against a darker background or whether they are silhouetted against a deep blue sky, the main note, causing that impression of unity, is the parallelism of the trunks. If you look at a field in which only one species of flower is in evidence, dandelions for instance, which stand out yellow against the green background of the grass, you receive an impression of unity which delights you. The effect will be greater, the impression stronger than any diversity, unless that diversity has a framework of parallelism. Imagine now a path lined with laurels, or flowering lilac all the same color: you will feel the charm of repetition. Picture yourself in the middle of a wide expanse of ground covered with rocks fallen from a mountain side: you will have the same feeling, but even stronger because of the very nature of things. High in the Alps, all the innumerable mountains surrounding us produce a similar impression, even more striking because the repetition is on a large scale. In the autumn, you see tree leaves—the same leaf, an acacia leaf for instance—scattered over the ground: their repetition causes a delightful impression.

If I look up at the sky, the uniformity of all its parts fills me with admiration. I could multiply such instances.

When it is not the main note, parallelism is an element of order. The symmetry of left and right in the human body, the symmetrical opposition which Michelangelo first used, then Raphael—that too is an instance of parallelism. In the clothes which cover our bodies, do we not have the same folds on both shoulders, the same folds on both elbows, and on both knees similar marks of our movements?

If we compare these decorative instances with occurrences from our daily life, we again find the principle of parallelism. We know, and we all feel at times, that what unites us is stronger than what divides us. If there is a public festival, you see everybody walking in the same direction. On other occasions, they are all grouped round a speaker who represents an idea. Walk into a church during a religious service: the feeling of unity will impress you. When we are gathered for a happy celebration, we do not like to be disturbed by a dissenting voice. In all the examples given, it is easy to see a common principle and to understand that the parallelism of the events is at the same time a decorative parallelism.

To aim at unity, at a strong and powerful unity, is to stress one thing above all others, to express it strongly, whether it is a graceful or a powerful subject. But that is not all. The present period proves it. There is a general mad rush toward diversity, except a few, who, like Puvis de Chavannes, introduce this harmonious note. Diversity is an element of beauty too, but it must not be exaggerated. The very fact of our having a point of view introduces diversity in a subject of absolute unity. The artist knows that: as soon as he wants to maintain the unity of his subject, he comes against the law of perspective which requires, for instance, that the apparent height of a man should diminish the farther he is from our eye. Look at three or four men walking with a similar movement. Their very physiognomic differences constitute a great variety. It is not always as easy as it seems to produce something simple.

I have said that a trained eye is better able than another to see the phenomena of light and form, but that it also needs the help of other instruments to understand the beauty of the body. But the best instrument of all is the human brain which, through its faculty of comparing one harmony to another, finds out their real relationship:—that activity of the brain, allied with feelings from the heart, create new beauties. The work of art reveals a newly apprehended order of things and is beautiful because it expresses a general harmony.

Winter 1896-1897.

Notes

[1]Manuscript: Fribourg; Bibliothèque des Arts et Métiers. The manuscript is dated, although not from Hodler's hand, "Winter 1896-97"; but the title "The Mission of the Artist" does not appear at the top of the manuscript. The subtitles "Color" and "The Work of Art" are by Hodler.

The whole manuscript has been heavily corrected and crossed out, partly by Hodler himself, partly too by one or perhaps several other hands. Hodler wrote this lecture at the request of the Director of the Musée Industriel of Fribourg, Léon Genoud, who had also asked him to give a course on painting in the same town. The Fribourg lecture has been published several times, most notably and for the first time in the newspaper *La Liberté*, Fribourg, March 18, 19, and 20, 1897. A comparison of the published text with the original manuscript shows that the corrections by a strange hand were made by the editor of that newspaper. For instance, the subtitle "Form" was introduced by the copy editor of *La Liberté*. Other changes occurred in proof form, among which was the adding of the subtitle "The Eye," so that the version printed by the newspaper finally contained several variants from Hodler's manuscript. Ewald Bender published the Fribourg lecture (in: *Die Kunst Ferdinand Holders*, Zurich, 1923, p. 231ff.), after the text published in *La Liberté* quoted above; but he is the first to introduce the title "The Mission of the Artist" which, in fact, only takes up the first words of the lecture. C. A. Loosli meant to give "the first original version, based on Hodler's manuscript" (in: *Ferdinand Holder—Leben, Werk und Nachlass*, Bern, 1921-24, vol. IV, p. 299ff.), but the text he has established is so full of mistakes that it is useless as the basis of a translation. For this first English translation, we have used the original French text by Hodler. But we have kept the title "The Mission of the Artist" given by Bender and also the subtitles introduced by the editor of *La Liberté*. We have also maintained the minor corrections made by the copy editor of that newspaper whenever they help to make the meaning clearer. To avoid overloading the text with notes, and since this is not a scientific publication of the script, we have not attempted to mention in the footnotes all the passages crossed out by Hodler, all the corrections by another hand, nor all variants appearing in the other publications of "The Mission of the Artist" which we have mentioned here. 'Professor André Hurst, of the University of Geneva, does not believe that this quotation is a literal transcription from Plato, but rather a paraphrase from one of several sources, either from *The Phaido, The Republic*, or *The Banquet*. According to evidence (C. A. Loosli, *Ferdinand Hodler—Leben, Werk und Nachlass*, Bern, 1921-1924, vol. I, p. 235), Hodler had read Plato's *The Banquet*, which inspired in 1876 "The Banquet of Gymnasts," the cartoon of which was destroyed, and the painted version of which is in the Kunsthaus Zurich (both are reproduced in: Jura Brüschweiler, *Ferdinand Hodler—Anthologie critique*, Lausanne, 1971, p. 23).

Emil Orlik (Germany, 1870–1932). *Portrait
of Ferdinand Hodler.* 1904. Woodcut. 14 x
9⅝". University Art Museum, Berkeley. [Not
in exhibition.]

Chronology

Compiled by Jura Brüschweiler

1853
March 14, birth of Ferdinand Hodler in Bern, oldest of six children. His father, Johann Hodler from Gurzelen (Canton of Bern) was a carpenter; his mother, Margarete, née Neukomm, earned a living as a cook and laundress.

1859
Family moves to La Chaux-de-Fonds (Canton of Bern). Hodler attends elementary school.

1860
Johann Hodler, bankrupt, dies at the age of 32 of tuberculosis.

1861
Hodler's mother marries Gottlieb Schüpbach, a commercial painter and a widower with three children. Three more children are to be born to them. (Between 1861 and 1885 all of Hodler's brothers and his sister die of tuberculosis.)

1862-1865
Elementary school in Bern. Assists stepfather in paint workshop.

1865-1867
Secondary school in Steffisburg, where Hodler's stepfather moved because of business failure. Paints signs. Death of Hodler's mother, spring of 1867 (age 39).

1868-1870
In Thun, Hodler is apprenticed to Ferdinand Sommer, a German painter of views for tourists.

1870
Hodler is in Langenthal (Canton of Bern).

1871
Stepfather Schüpbach emigrates to Boston, where he dies two years later.

1872
Hodler moves to Geneva, where he will live until the end of his life. Stays with the French composer Henri Giroud. At the Musée Rath, copies the paintings of Alexandre Calame and François Diday, two renowned Swiss nineteenth-century painters of mountain landscapes. Becomes the pupil of Barthélemy Menn at the Ecole des Beaux-Arts.

1873
Receives prize for clay modeling at the Ecole des Beaux-Arts.

1874
Finds a home with Frank de Morsier, an art patron. First theoretical writings. Prize at the Calame competition for his painting.

1875
Trip to Basel. Admires Holbein at the Kunstmuseum in Basel. Audits courses at the high school (collège) in Geneva. Studies Dürer's theory of proportions with Menn.

1877
Military service in Swiss Infantry.

1878
Trip to Spain; visits the Prado in Madrid.

1879
Remains in Madrid until June; returns to Geneva.

1880
Paints religious compositions.

1881
Takes a studio in Geneva at Grand'Rue 35. Exhibits *The Angry One* at the Salon in Paris. In May, visits Langenthal. Makes a trip to Lyon, France, where he assists in painting two "Panoramas."

1882
Six-month stay in Langenthal. In Geneva, hears lecture on Egyptian art and symbolism in art.

1883
Trip to Munich, where Hodler is impressed by Dürer's work in the Pinakothek.

1884
Meets Augustine Dupin, a seamstress from Geneva. Their liaison lasts over several years.

1885
First one-man exhibition at the Cercle des Beaux-Arts, Geneva. Weekly meetings with painters and poets in Hodler's studio, among these the symbolist poet Louis Duchosal. *Beech Forest* is his first Parallelist landscape.

1886
Cycle of decorative paintings illustrating a local historical event for the Taverne du Crocodile in Geneva.

1887
One-man exhibition at the Kunstmuseum in Bern. Birth of Hector, Hodler's son with Augustine Dupin. Kunstmuseum Bern acquires *The Angry One.*

1889
Hodler marries Berta Stucki. Receives an honorable mention for *Procession of Wrestlers* at the Paris World's Fair.

1890
Paints *Night*, his first large-scale, symbolical composition. Competes for two mural designs commissioned by the Swiss Federal Institute of Technology.

1891
At the order of the mayor of Geneva, *Night* is withdrawn from a municipal exhibition. It is shown in Paris, at the Salon du Champ-de-Mars presided over by Puvis de Chavannes. Hodler becomes a member of the Société Nationale des Artistes Français (president, Puvis de Chavannes). Divorces Berta Stucki.

1892
The Disillusioned is shown at the Salon de la Rose†Croix Esthétique, in Paris. Hodler becomes a member of the society.

1893
Stay in the Tessin. Hodler wins second prize at the Calame competition for *Autumn Evening*. *Communion with Infinite* exhibited at the Salon du Champ-de-Mars in Paris.

1894
Exhibits *Night* in Kunstpalast, Berlin; *The Chosen One* exhibited at the Salon du

Champ-de-Mars, Paris. Two large murals are shown at the Antwerp World's Fair. Returns to Geneva by way of Brussels and Paris.

1895

Eurythmy exhibited at the Salon du Champ-de-Mars, Paris. Second prize, Calame competition, for *Lake Geneva from Chexbres*.

1896

Exhibits 22 large-scale, single-figure paintings at the Swiss National Fair in Geneva. *Night* excluded from exhibition. Swiss Confederation acquires *Procession of Wrestlers*. City of Geneva acquires *Angry Warrior*. Teaches painting and drawing at the Musée des Arts Decoratifs in Fribourg, until 1899.

1897

Receives first prize at a competition sponsored by the state for the Schweizerisches Landesmuseum in Zurich for *The Retreat from Marignano*. The museum's director opposes the decision of the jury. A vehement campaign ensues, lasting three years. Hodler revises his design, which now is in the place originally intended. Hodler lectures on "The Mission of the Artist" in Fribourg. Receives a gold medal at the International Exhibition in Munich for *Night* and *Eurythmy*. Becomes a member of the Society of Swiss Painters, Sculptors, and Architects.

1898

Remains in Bern for almost a year, working on the design for *The Retreat from Marignano*. Marries the twenty-nine-year-old school mistress Berthe Jacques of Geneva. Beginning of friendship with painter Cuno Amiet, friend of Gauguin. The Swiss Confederation acquires *Avalanche*.

1899

Night and *The Disillusioned* are shown at the III Biennale in Venice.

1900

Executes *The Retreat from Marignano* fresco at the Schweizerisches Landesmuseum in Zurich. Visits Paris. *Night*, *Eurythmy*, and *Day*, exhibited at the Paris World's Fair, receive the gold medal. Becomes member of the Vienna and Berlin Secessions.

1901

Participates in the Salon de la Libre Esthétique in Brussels. The Kunstmuseum, Bern, acquires *Night*, *The Disillusioned*, and *Day*; the Kunstmuseum, Winterthur, acquires *Tired of Life*, *Spring*, and *The Chosen* at the exhibition of the Vienna Secession; the Kunsthistorisches Museum, Vienna, acquires *Emotion*.

1903

Hodler stays in Vienna, where he copies his own work, *The Chosen*, now at the Municipal Museum of Hagen/Westphalia. Participates in group shows in Munich, Venice, and Berlin.

1904

Thirty-one paintings exhibited at the Vienna

Secession establish his European reputation. Encounters Gustav Klimt, Josef Hoffmann, Franz Servaes. Baron von Reininghaus purchases several large paintings. Two trips to Vienna. Hodler becomes a member of the Munich Secession and of the German Society of Artists in Berlin.

1905

First voyage to Italy. Impressed by Giotto in Florence. Trip to Berlin, where he encounters Lovis Corinth. Hodler and Klimt exhibit together at the Berlin Secession.

1906

Important one-man exhibition in Zurich.

1907

The Society of the Friends of Art of Jena and Weimar commissions Hodler to design a mural for the University of Jena. The Musée d'Art et d'Histoire in Geneva acquires the final oil study for *The Retreat from Marignano*. One-man show of Hodler's works at Galerie Cassirer in Berlin.

1908

Hodler stays in Jena, where he works on the mural; in Frankfurt for a group show of Swiss painters; in Dresden, where he becomes a member of the prize jury of the German Society of Artists; in the Bernese Oberland, where he paints a series of landscapes. Becomes president of the Society of Swiss Painters, Sculptors, and Architects.

1909

Hodler meets Valentine Godé-Darel. With M. Buri organizes an international art exhibition in Interlaken, in which Max Liebermann and Joseph Toorop participate. Publicly defends the painter Félix Vallotton, heavily criticized in Zurich. Death of Augustine Dupin.

1910

A Doctorate of Honor conferred on Hodler by the University of Basel. With other Swiss painters, he exhibits at the Nemzeti Szalon in Budapest.

1911

At the recommendation of Max Liebermann, the City of Hannover commissions Hodler to do a mural for the town hall (*Unanimity*). Sojourns in Berlin (made honorary member of the Secession), Hannover, Rome (on the prize jury for the International Exhibition). Retrospective exhibitions in Cologne, Frankfurt am Main, Basel, Zurich, Munich, and Berlin. Swiss bank notes carry vignettes after two Hodler works. Emil Orlik with Hodler in Chexbres.

1912

Becomes member of the Academy of Arts in Dresden.

1913

To Hannover for opening of new town hall. Exhibits as the featured artist at the Salon d'Automne in Paris. Among his paintings: second version of *Unanimity*. On this occasion he is made Officer of the Legion of Honor. A banquet is held in his honor in Paris. He meets Rodin. Exhibits at the International Exhibition in Munich. Birth of Pauline Valentine, his daughter with Valentine Godé-Darel.

1914

Moves into an apartment designed by Austrian architect Josef Hoffmann (29 Quai du Mont Blanc, Geneva). With other Swiss intellectuals, signs a protest against the German bombardment of Reims Cathedral. As a result, is expelled from all the German art societies of which he was a member.

1915

Death of Valentine Godé-Darel. Hodler meets and portrays Carl Spitteler. Jawlensky visits Hodler in Geneva.

1916

Designated Honorary Professor at the Ecole des Beaux-Arts in Geneva, where he teaches drawing until June, 1917. Sojourn in Montana to be near his son Hector, ill with tuberculosis. Series of self-portraits.

1917

Large retrospective exhibition at the Kunsthaus in Zurich. Becomes ill with lung edema.

1918

Made honorary citizen of Geneva. Suffers a relapse of his illness. Paints a series of Mont Blanc landscapes from the window of his sickroom. Hodler dies in Geneva on May 19. Buried at the cemetery of Saint-Georges.

Selected Bibliography

by Jura Brüschweiler

I. *Monographs*

Bender, Ewald: *Das Leben Ferdinand Hodlers.* (With contributions by H. Bahr, R. Breuer, and P. Modrow.) Zurich, 1921. (French edition: Zurich, 1923.)

Bender, Ewald: *Die Kunst Ferdinand Hodlers* (1st Vol.). Zurich, 1923. (2nd Vol., see, W.Y. Müller: *Die Kunst Ferdinand Hodlers.* Zurich, 1941.)

Brüschweiler, Jura: *Ferdinand Hodler— Anthologie critique.* Lausanne, 1971. (German edition: Lausanne, 1970.)

Burger, Fritz: *Cézanne und Hodler.* Munich, 1913.

Frey, Adolf: *Ferdinand Hodler.* Leipzig, 1922.

Guerzoni, Stéphanie: *Ferdinand Hodler—Sa Vie, son Oeuvre, son Enseignement, Souvenirs Personnels.* Geneva, 1957. (German edition: Zurich, 1958.)

Hugelshofer, Walter: *Ferdinand Hodler.* Zurich, 1952.

Klein, Rudolf: *Ferdinand Hodler et les Suisses.* Paris, n.d. [1909]. (English edition: London, n.d. [1909].) (German edition: [Berlin, 1909].)

Loosli, Charles-Albert: *Ferdinand Hodler* (Mappenwerk und Textband). Zurich, 1919-1921. (French edition of text: Zurich, 1922.)

Loosli, Charles-Albert: *Ferdinand Hodler— Leben, Werk und Nachlass,* (4 Vols.). Bern, 1921-1924. (Vol. 4 contains a "catalogue raisonné" of Hodler's works.)

Loosli, Charles-Albert: *Ferdinand Hodler.* Paris, 1931.

Loosli, Charles-Albert: *Aus der Werkstatt Ferdinand Hodlers.* Basel, 1938.

Mühlestein, Hans: *Ferdinand Hodler—Ein Deutungsversuch.* Weimar, 1914.

Mühlestein, Hans, and Schmidt, Georg: *Ferdinand Hodler, 1853-1918, sein Leben und sein Werk.* Erlenbach/Zurich, 1942.

Müller, Werner Y.: *Die Kunst Ferdinand Hodlers. Reife und Spätwerk.* (2nd Vol. of E. Bender: *Die Kunst Ferdinand Hodlers.* Zurich, 1941.)

Roffler, Thomas: *Ferdinand Hodler.* Frauenfeld and Leipzig, 1926.

Uberwasser, Walter: *Ferdinand Hodler—Köpfe und Gestalten.* (Photography by Robert Spreng.) Zurich, 1947.

Weese, Arthur: *Ferdinand Hodler.* Bern, 1910.

II. *Special Studies*

Angst, Heinrich: *Die Wandmalereien in der Waffenhalle des Schweizerischen Landesmuseums.* Zurich, 1900.

Ankwicz-Kleehofen, Hans, Cuno Amiet, and Kolomann Moser: "Hodler und Wien." *Neujahrsblatt der Zürcher Kunstgesellschaft 1950.* Zurich, 1950.

Baud-Bovy, Daniel: *Les Hodlers au Musée d'Art et d'Histoire de Genève.* (Introduction by Waldemar Deonna.) Geneva, 1940.

Brüschweiler, Jura: "Ferdinand Hodler und sein Sohn Hector." *Neujahrsblatt der Zürcher Kunstgesellschaft 1966/1967.* Zurich, 1967.

Godet, Pierre: *Hodler.* Neuchatel, 1921.

Graef, Botho: *Hodlers und Hoffmanns Wandbilder in der Universität Jena.* Jena, 1910.

Hercourt, Jean: *Trois essais: Ferdinand Hodler, C. F. Ramuz, André Gide.* La Chaux-de-Fonds, 1942.

Hilber, Baud-Bovy, Loosli: *Hodler. Ein zeitgenössisches Dokument.* (With photographs of the artist.) Bern, 1943.

Kesser, Hans: *Zeichnungen Ferdinand Hodlers.* (Postscript by F. Baur.) Basel, 1921.

Maeder, Alphonse: *Ferdinand Hodler. Eine*

Skizze seiner Seelischen Entwicklung und Bedeutung für die schweizerische-nationale Kultur. Zurich, 1916.
(French edition: Geneva, 1916.)

Russ, Willy: *Mes souvenirs sur Ferdinand Hodler.* Lausanne, 1945.

Steiger, Günther: *Fall Hodler. Jena 1914-1919, Der Kampf um ein Gemälde.* (With contributions by G. Steiger, F. Bolck, F. Möbius, W. Victor, L. Poethe, B. Wächter, and the assistance of O. Köhler.) Jena, Friedrich-Schiller-Universität, 1970.

Steinberg, S. D.: *Ferdinand Hodler—Ein Platoniker der Kunst/Ein Versuch.* Zurich, 1919.

Trog, Hans: *Ferdinand Hodler—Erinnerung an die Hodler-Ausstellung im Zürcher Kunsthaus, Sommer 1917.* Zurich, 1918.

von Tavel, Hans Christoph: *Ferdinand Hodler— "Die Nacht."* Stuttgart, 1969.

Wartmann, Wilhelm: "Hodler in Zürich." *Neujahrsblatt der Zürcher Kunstgesellschaft 1919.*

Waser, Maria: *Wege zu Hodler.* Zurich, 1927.

Weese, Arthur: *Aus der Welt Ferdinand Hodlers—Sein Werdegang auf Grund der Sommerausstellung 1917 im Zürcher Kunsthaus.* Bern, 1918.

Widmann, Fritz: *Erinnerungen an Ferdinand Hodler.* Zurich, 1918.

Widmer, Johannes: *Von Hodlers letztem Lebensjahr.* Zurich, 1919.

Widmer, Johannes: *Les Hodler de la Collection Russ-Young.* Geneva. 1925.

III. Dissertations

Dietschi, Peter: *Der Parallelismus Ferdinand Hodlers, Ein Beitrag zur Stilpsychologie der neueren Kunst.* Basler Studien zur Kunstgeschichte Vol. 16. Basel, 1957.

Müller, Werner Y.: *Ferdinand Hodler als Landschaftsmaler.* Diss. Phil. Fak. I. University of Zurich. Glarus, 1940.
(cf.: *Die Kunst Ferdinand Hodlers.* Zurich, 1941.)

Portmann, Paul: *Kompositionsgesetze in der Malerei von Ferdinand Hodler, nachgewiesen an den Figurengruppen von 1890-1918.* Diss. Phil. Fak. I. University of Zurich. Winterthur, 1956.

Schmid, Ernst Heinrich: *Ferdinand Hodlers "Rückzug bei Marignano" im Waffensaal des Landesmuseums Zürich—Ein Beitrag zur Geschichte des schweizerischen Wandbildes.* Diss. Phil. Fak. I. University of Zurich. Affoltern a. A. 1946.

IV. Exhibition Catalogues

Frankfurt 1911. *Hodler-Ausstellung.* Frankfurter Kunstverein. (Preface by Robert Schwerdtfeger.)

Munich 1911. *Kollektiv-Ausstellung Ferd. Hodler.* Moderne Galerie Heinrich Thannhauser.

Paris 1913. *Exposition de Ferdinand Hodler.* Salon d'Automne. (Preface by Mathias Morhardt.)

Zurich 1917. *Ausstellung Ferdinand Hodler.* Kunsthaus Zurich. (Preface by W. Wartmann.)

Geneva 1918. *Exposition Ferdinand Hodler.* Galerie Moos. (Preface by J. Widmer, C. A. Loosli, and L. Florentin.)

Bern 1921. *Hodler Gedächtnis-Ausstellung.* Kunstmuseum Bern. (Preface by C. von Mandach.)

Winterthur 1932. *Der frühe Hodler.* Museum Winterthur. (Preface by Hans R. Hahnloser.)

Bern 1938. *Ferdinand Hodler—Gedächtnis-Ausstellung.* Kunstmuseum Bern. (Preface by C. von Mandach.)

New York 1940. *Ferdinand Hodler.* Durand-Ruel Galleries. (Preface by Charlotte Weidler.)

Zurich 1951. *Hodler als Historienmaler.* Helmhaus Zurich. (Preface by Landolt and W. Y. Müller.)

Thun 1953. *Ausstellung Ferdinand Hodler, 1853-1918.* Kunstmuseum der Stadt Thun, Thunerhof.

St. Gallen 1953. *Ferdinand Hodler 1853-1918.* Kunstmuseum St. Gallen. (Preface by R. Suter and R. Hanhart.)

Pro Helvetia 1954. *F. Hodler.* Traveling exhibition organized by the Pro Helvetia Foundation in Zurich, exhibited in Cologne, Munich, and Hamburg. (Introduction by J. R. von Salis, explanatory remarks by Walter Hugelshofer.)

Biel 1956. *Ferdinand Hodler.* Städtische Galerie. (Preface by H. Kern, J.-P. Pellaton, and R. Schindler.)

Vienna 1962/1963. *Ferdinand Hodler 1853-1918.* Vienna Secession. (Catalogue by Jura Brüschweiler, preface by Walter Hugelshofer.)

Geneva 1963. *Ferdinand Hodler, Dessins.* Musée Rath. (Preface by Jura Brüschweiler and Pierre Bouffard.)

Zurich 1963. *Ferdinand Hodler, Zeichnungen.* Helmhaus Zurich. (Preface by Eduard Hüttinger and Jura Brüschweiler.)

Zurich 1964. *Ferdinand Hodler, Landschaften der Reife and Spätzeit.* Kunsthaus Zurich. (Preface by E. Hüttinger and J. Brüschweiler, texts by W. F. Burger and M. Barraud.)

Bern 1968. *Ferdinand Hodler.* Exhibition for the 50th anniversary of his death. Kunstmuseum Bern. (Preface by Hugo Wagner.)

London 1971. *Ferdinand Hodler.* Hayward Gallery. (Preface by Hugo Wagner.)

Catalogue to the Exhibition

Dimensions are in inches, height preceding width, except where otherwise noted. Dates enclosed in parentheses do not appear on works. Illustrated works are indicated with an asterisk. Except as noted in individual entries, all works are included in all showings of the exhibition. All titles and dates were established by Jura Brüschweiler.

Paintings:

*1. *The Student.* 1874. Oil on canvas. 44½ x 28¾". Kunsthaus Zurich. [Ill. p. 17.]

2. *Portrait of Miss Caroline Leschaud.* 1874. Oil on canvas. 44½ x 28". Kunsthaus Zurich.

*3. *Watchmaker Workshop Madrid.* (1879). Oil on canvas. 32¼ x 36⅝". Kunstmuseum Lucerne (extended loan from Gottfried Keller Foundation). [Ill. p. 19.]

*4. *On the Shore of the Manzanares River near Madrid.* (1879). Oil on canvas. 17⅜ x 25⅝". Musée d'Art et d'Histoire, Geneva. [Ill. p. 21.]

*5. *The Angry One.* (1881). Oil on canvas. 28½ x 20¾". Kunstmuseum Bern. [Ill. p. 23]

6. *The Small "Prayer".* (1881–1882). Oil on canvas. 32¾ x 39⅜". Collection Dr. Max Schmidheiny, Heerbrugg.

7. *Reading Craftsman (Shoemaker Fritz Neukomm, Hodler's Uncle).* (1882). Oil on canvas. 14½ x 10". Oeffentliche Kunstsammlung Basel.

*8. *Portrait of Louise-Delphine Duchosal.* (1885). Oil on canvas. 21⅝ x 18⅛". Kunsthaus Zurich. [Ill. p. 25.]

*9. *Beech Forest.* 1885. Oil on canvas. 39¾ x 51½". Museum der Stadt Solothurn. [Ill. p. 27.]

10. *Pregnant Woman.* (1887). Oil on canvas. 28⅛ x 20⅛". Kunstmuseum Bern (extended loan from Gottfried Keller Foundation).

11. *The Chestnut Trees.* 1889. Oil on canvas. 18½ x 12⅝". Musée d'Art et d'Histoire, Geneva.

*12. *Mother and Child.* (ca. 1889). Oil on canvas. 14⅛ x 11". Collection Professor Hans R. Hahnloser, Bern. [Ill. p. 29.]

13. *Girl with Poppy.* (ca. 1890). Oil on canvas. 25⅝ x 15¾". Kunstmuseum Bern (extended loan from Gottfried Keller Foundation).

*14. *Night.* (1890). Oil on canvas. 45¾ x 117¾". Kunstmuseum Bern. [New York showing only.] [Ill. p. 31.]

15. *Self-portrait.* 1891. Oil on canvas. 11¼ x 9". Musée d'Art et d'Histoire, Geneva (extended loan from Gottfried Keller Foundation).

*16. *Autumn Evening.* (1892). Oil on canvas. 39⅜ x 51¼". Musée d'Art et d'Histoire, Neuchatel. [Ill. p. 43.]

*17. *The Disillusioned.* 1892. Oil on canvas. 47¼ x 117¾". Kunstmuseum Bern. [Ill. p. 33.]

*18. *Disillusioned One.* 1892. Oil on canvas. 21¾ x 17½". Collection B. Gerald Cantor, Beverly Hills, California. [Ill. p. 35.]

19. *Lake Shore, Maggia Delta.* (1893). Oil on canvas. 15¾ x 23⅝". Kunsthaus Zurich.

20. *Shore of Lake Lugano.* (1893). Oil on canvas. 30 x 18⅛". Private Collection, Worben.

21. *Emotion (Model: Berthe Jacques, Hodler's Future Wife).* 1894. Oil on canvas. 17¾ x 10¼". Kunstmuseum Bern.

*22. *Eurythmy.* 1895. Oil on canvas. 65¾ x 96½". Kunstmuseum Bern. [Ill. p. 37.]

*23. *Lake Geneva from Chexbres.* (1895). Oil on canvas. 39⅜ x 51¼". Kunsthaus Zurich (extended loan from Gottfried Keller Foundation). [Ill. p. 45.]

*24. *Wounded Warrior* (study for the left part of the fresco, *The Retreat from Marignano,* in the Schweizerisches Landesmuseum, Zurich). (1897). Oil on canvas. 78½ x 68⅞". Musée d'Art et d'Histoire, Geneva. [Ill. p. 61.]

*25. *Truth II.* (1903). Oil on canvas. 81⅞ x 116⅛". Kunsthaus Zurich. [Ill. p. 41.]

*26. *Day II.* (1904–1906). Oil on canvas. 64¼ x 141". Kunsthaus Zurich. [Berkeley showing only.] [Ill. p. 39.]

27. *Forest Brook.* 1904. Oil on canvas. 34⅞ x 39¾". Kunsthaus Zurich.

28. *Lake Geneva from Chexbres.* 1905. Oil on canvas. 31½ x 39½". Musée d'Art et d'Histoire, Geneva.

*29. *Lake Geneva from Chexbres.* (1906–1908). Oil on canvas. 31½ x 50¾". Collection Kurt Meissner, Zurich. [Ill. p. 47.]

30. *Lake Silvaplana.* 1907. Oil on canvas. Private Collection, Switzerland. [New York showing only.]

31. *Eiger, Mönch, and Jungfrau in Morning Fog.* 1908. Oil on canvas. Collection Dr. A. Gerber, Zurich.

*32. *Eiger, Mönch, and Jungfrau in Moonlight.* (1908). Oil on canvas. 28⅜ x 26⅜". Collection Josef Müller, Solothurn. [Ill. p. 53 and cover.]

33. *Landscape near Chateau-d'Oex.* (ca. 1908?). Oil on canvas. 28⅜ x 33". Private Collection, Switzerland.

34. *Portrait of Jeanne Cerani-Charles.* (1908/1911). Oil on canvas. 16⅛ x 11¾". Private Collection, Geneva.

*35. *Augustine Dupin on her Deathbed.* 1909. Oil on canvas. 29¾ x 35½". Museum der Stadt Solothurn (Dübi-Müller Foundation). [Ill. p. 63.]

*36. *Lake Thun.* 1909. Oil on canvas. 26½ x 36¼". Musée d'Art et d'Histoire, Geneva. [Ill. p. 49.]

37. *Bernese Alps before Sunrise.* (1908/1911). Oil on canvas. 22 x 14½". Collection Mr. and Mrs. Robert M. Schwarzenbach, Norwalk, Connecticut.

*38. *Niesen.* (1910). Oil on canvas. 32¾ x 41½".

Oeffentliche Kunstsammlung Basel. [Ill. p. 55.]

39. *Portrait of the Model Giulia Leonardi*. 1910. Oil on canvas. 15½ x 11¾″. Oeffentliche Kunstsammlung Basel.

40. *Portrait of Jeanne Cerani-Charles*. (ca. 1910). Oil on canvas. 21⅝ x 15¼″. The Detroit Institute of Arts (City Purchase).

*41. *Breithorn*. (1911). Oil on canvas. 26⅜ x 35″. Kunstmuseum Lucerne (extended loan from Bernhard Eglin Foundation). [Ill. p. 57.]

42. *Portrait of Valentine Godé-Darel*. (1911). Oil on canvas. 17 x 13″. Kunsthaus Zurich.

43. *Woman in Ecstasy (Model: Giulia Leonardi)*. 1911. Oil on canvas. 66½ x 33½″. Private Collection, Bern.

44. *Woman in Ecstasy*. 1911. Oil on canvas. 67¾ x 33⅝″. Musée d'Art et d'Histoire, Geneva.

45. *Grand Muveran*. 1912. Oil on canvas. 25⅝ x 33½″. Collection Josef Müller, Solothurn.

46. *Mountains near Grindelwald*. (1912). Oil on canvas. 33½ x 31½″. Kunsthaus Zurich.

*47. *Self-portrait*. (1912). Oil on canvas. 13¼ x 10⅝″. Kunstmuseum Winterthur. [Ill. p. 67.]

48. *Portrait of Mathias Morhardt*. 1913. Oil on canvas. 33⅝ x 24⅞″. Musée d'Art et d'Histoire, Geneva.

49. *Jungfrau in Snow*. 1914. Oil on canvas. 20½ x 28⅜″. Collection Messrs. Maus & Nordmann, Geneva.

50. *Mönch*. 1914. Oil on canvas. 24⅜ x 33⅞″. Kunstmuseum Olten.

*51. *Self-portrait*. 1914. Oil on canvas. 16¾ x 15⅛″. Museum zu Allerheiligen Schaffhausen. [Ill. p. 67.]

*52. *The Sick Valentine Godé-Darel*. 1914. Oil on canvas. 24¾ x 33½″. Collection Mrs. Gertrud Dübi, Solothurn. [Ill. p. 65.]

53. *The Dying Valentine Godé-Darel*. 1915. Oil on canvas. 23⅞ x 35⅝″. Oeffentliche Kunstsammlung Basel.

54. *Lake Geneva after Sunset*. (1915). Oil on paper. 18⅞ x 24¾″. Collection Josef Müller, Solothurn.

55. *Mme. Godé-Darel, Dying*. (1915). Oil on paper. 13⅜ x 19¼″. Kunstmuseum St. Gallen (Sturzenegger Collection).

56. *Portrait of James Vibert*. 1915. Oil on canvas. 25⅝ x 18⅛″. Musée d'Art et d'Histoire, Geneva.

*57. *Sunset at Lake Geneva*. (1915). Oil on canvas. 24 x 35½″. Kunsthaus Zurich. [Ill. p. 46.]

58. *Brook near Champery*. 1916. Oil on canvas. 23⅝ x 31⅛″. Collection J. J. Kurz, Zurich.

*59. *Self-portrait*. 1916. Oil on canvas. 15¾ x 15″. Musée d'Art et d'Histoire, Geneva. [Ill. p. 67.]

60. *Portrait of the Swedish Writer Frederick Robert Martin*. (1916–1917). Oil on canvas.

36¼ x 31½″. Kunsthaus Zurich.

61. *Lake Geneva from Caux*. (1917). Oil on canvas. 25⅝ x 31⅞″. Collection Josef Müller, Solothurn.

*62. *Landscape near Caux with Rising Clouds*. 1917. Oil on canvas. 25¾ x 31⅞″. Kunsthaus Zurich. [Ill. p. 59.]

*63. *Self-portrait*. (1917). Oil on board mounted on canvas. 15¼ x 12⅜″. Musée d'Art et d'Histoire, Geneva. [Ill. p. 12.]

*64. *Self-portrait*. (1917–1918). Oil on board. 16⅞ x 13″. Musée d'Art et d'Histoire, Geneva. [Ill. p. 69.]

65. *Lake Geneva with Mont Blanc before Sunrise*. 1918. Oil on canvas. 25⅝ x 31⅞″. Collection Josef Müller, Solothurn.

66. *Mont Blanc Chain in Foggy Weather*. 1918. Oil on canvas. 23⅝ x 31½″. Private Collection, Geneva.

*67. *The Shore of Lake Geneva at Dawn*. (1918). Oil on canvas. 24⅛ x 50⅜″. Musée d'Art et d'Histoire, Geneva. [Ill. p. 47.]

Drawings:

Catalogue entries prepared by Phyllis Hattis, in consultation with Jura Brüschweiler. Note that in these entries the bibliographical reference gives only the single most accessible source of publication for each drawing.

*68. *Lake Brienz*. (ca. 1870). Brush and watercolor on cream wove paper. 5⅛ x 8¼″. Collection Rudolf-Emil Schindler, Ligerz. [Ill. p. 85.]
Unsigned. Dry estate stamp in lower right.
Reference: Jura Brüschweiler, *Ferdinand Hodler Dessins*, Musée Rath, 1963, no. 2.
This postcard-sized landscape, one of Hodler's earliest known works, derives its compositional tenets from late eighteenth- and early nineteenth-century Swiss and German landscape painting (cf. the work of Calame and Diday).

*69. *Bull*. (1878–1879). Pen and ink over graphite underdrawing on tan paper. 5⅛ x 6″. Kunsthaus Zurich (Hodler Archives no. 1005). [Ill. p. 85.]
Signed and inscribed in graphite, by the artist: Madrid/F. Hodler.
Reference: Jura Brüschweiler, *Ferdinand Hodler Dessins*, Musée Rath, 1963, no. 8.
The form of the bull is defined by interlocking volumes, modulated within a closed, or open (as in the background bulls) angular contour. The degree of abstraction from a more fully modeled form, detailed to convince the viewer of the bull's three-dimensional character, connotes a cubist technique of rendering form through distinct, faceted, interconnected planes.

*70. *A Street of Madrid*. (1878–1879). Brown ink over hard graphite line of underdrawing on

cream wove paper, discolored with age.
7¼ x 4¼". Kunsthaus Zurich (Z Inv. 1919/22).
[Ill. p. 85.]
Unsigned.
Reference: Jura Brüschweiler, *Ferdinand Hodler Dessins*, Musée Rath, 1963, no. 10.
With a hard graphite tool, followed by a fine pen point, Hodler depicts a scene of perpendicular planes of architecture along a narrow city street. This sketch demonstrates Hodler's grasp of one-point perspective drawing.

*71. *Spanish Bar.* (1878–1879). Graphite with stumping on paper. 5¼ x 8⅛". Kunsthaus Zurich (Z Inv. 1964/24). [Ill. p. 85.]
Unsigned. Dry estate stamp in lower right.
Reference: Jura Brüschweiler, *Neujahrsblatt der Zurcher Kunstgesellschaft*, 1966/1967, p. 85 (see footnote 15 in Hattis essay).
In this drawing, Hodler varies his use of a graphite tool, first drawing with it, then rubbing over his lines with a soft stump, and finally accenting the middle tones achieved in the first two processes with erasure highlights and overdrawing to create dark tones. The drawing is a study composed of rectilinear planes and silhouetted forms.

72. *"La belle Augustine pensive."* (1884–1885).
Pen and china ink and wash over graphite underdrawing. 11¼ x 8¾". Kunstmuseum Bern (Bequest of Mme. Hector Hodler, 1964).
Unsigned. Inscribed above figure, by the artist: La belle Augustine pensive.
Unpublished.
In mood and style of rendering, this drawing exemplifies Hodler's early figure style. The female form has rounded contours, its parts ordered symmetrically. The graphic silhouette expresses the calm mood of the sitter.

73. *The Historian (a Self-portrait).* (1886).
Graphite underdrawing, with gouache, watercolor, and black ink, on brown wove paper. 7½ x 6⅜". Musée d'Art et d'Histoire, Geneva.
Unsigned.
Reference: Jura Brüschweiler, *Ferdinand Hodler Dessins*, Musée Rath, 1963, no. 28.
Hodler here portrays himself as an observer being observed, as a critic recording a person and mood, while being recorded. The drawing focuses on self-observation and self-criticism. The drawn study employs a flowing, continuous contour and curved line, a flexibility of pose and a sense of the immediacy of gaze, held within a specific moment in time. This is partly obscured in the subsequent full-scale painting in oil (now in a private collection in Basel).

*74. *Mother with Child.* (ca. 1888). Graphite with stumping on cream wove paper. 12½ x 19¼". Kunsthaus Zurich (Z Inv. 1964/34). [Ill. p. 87.]
Unsigned. Dry estate stamp in lower right corner.

Reference: Jura Brüschweiler, *Neujahrsblatt der Zurcher Kunstgesellschaft*, 1966/1967, p. 89, fig. 92.
This tonal study for the painted canvas of 1889 (Oskar Reinhart Foundation, Winterthur) extends the pictorial exercise in tone and silhouetted forms of no. 71 and applies this style of rendering to the human figure. The manner of setting a figure's silhouette off against a rectangular frame (the molding of the door at the rear wall) suggests the artist's familiarity with the portraits of Degas.

75. *Self-portrait.* (1886–1891). Graphite under pen and ink with china ink wash on cream-colored wove paper. 4½ x 5¾". Musée d'Art et d'Histoire, Geneva.
Signed, lower right, in pen and ink: F. Hodler.
Reference: Jura Brüschweiler, *Ferdinand Hodler Dessins*, Musée Rath, 1963, no. 42.
Hodler has reduced the narrative content of his earlier self-portrait, *The Historian* (no. 73), into a refined and simplified bust-view composition of tonal and linear contrasts, juxtaposing line to plane, and flat tonal areas to graded ones. With such different means, Hodler once again, as in no. 73, exposes himself as a highly intense, emotionally penetrating image. This self-portrait was painted in 1891 (now in the Musée d'Art et d'Histoire, Geneva).

*76. *The Disillusioned.* (1891–1892). Graphite and red-orange crayon on thin cream wove paper squared for transfer. 11⅞ x 6". Collection Kurt Meissner, Zurich (M-5). [Ill. p. 87.]
Signed in lower right, in graphite: F. Hodler.
Dry estate stamp, to right above signature.
Reference: Jura Brüschweiler, catalogue of Hodler drawings from the Meissner Collection, Zurich, in preparation.
The central figure, painted in three variations on the theme, in 1891 and 1892, is preparatory to the larger composition in Bern and Munich. Hodler focuses on the hands, which reflect the figure's state of being. His emotions are energized yet blocked by despair and conflict. Hodler depicts these hands, limp yet well-defined in form, with a heavily overdrawn contour, actively curved in short divisions, and interior lines, stumped and drawn. More tentatively delineated are the bones, the veins, and the pulled flesh.

77. *Berthe Jacques.* (ca. 1894). Crayon under pen and china ink on white paper. 14⅞ x 10". Kunsthaus Zurich (Z Inv. 1943/29).
Signed lower right, in pen and ink: F. Hodler.
Reference: Jura Brüschweiler, *Ferdinand Hodler Dessins*, Musée Rath, 1963, no. 106.
This portrait, of the woman who marries the artist in 1898 and serves as his key model, is one of the first known drawings to employ a linear, decorative scheme that rests close

to the picture's surface, while creating a formal, symmetrical image. This style of rendering is developed in drawings nos. 78 and 79 and reflects Hodler's adaptation of the line popularly used by his contemporaries throughout Europe ca. 1900, today identified with the style called *Art Nouveau* or *Jugendstil*.

78. *Albert Trachsel*. (1896–1897). Graphite, pen and ink with red watercolor on cream wove paper. 14¾ x 11⅜". Kunstmuseum Bern.
Signed, twice, in red watercolor and graphite, lower right: F. Hodler.
Reference: Jura Brüschweiler, *Ferdinand Hodler Dessins*, Musée Rath, 1963, no. 66 (subsequently revised in unpublished notes of Jura Brüschweiler).
Hodler's portrait of his friend, Albert Trachsel, architect and painter, was engraved by H. C. Forestier and published as the frontispiece in *Les Fêtes réelles*, Paris, 1897.

79. *Study for the Reclining Male Figure in "The Dream."* (1897). Graphite under pink and blue pastel (or crayon), squared, on gray laid paper. 5¾ x 14⅝". Oeffentliche Kunstsammlung Basel (Kupferstichkabinett).
Signed, lower right, in black ink: F. Hodler.
Reference: Jura Brüschweiler, *Ferdinand Hodler Dessins*, Musée Rath, 1963, no. 148.
This study for a writhing male form, enveloped by the echoing magenta pastel lines extending laterally, employs a line that is no longer the calm, continuous contour of Hodler's earlier figure style. It is now agitated, vibrating, expressive of movement and emotional discontent. In the poster design, this male form becomes stabilized by its firmly controlled, more continuous contour.

80. *Poetry*. (1897). Graphite under crayon, gouache, and pen and ink, on brown wove paper mounted on canvas. 38⅝ x 27⅛". Kunstgewerbemuseum, Zurich.
Signed in graphite and red paint, lower right: Hodler.
Reference: Jura Brüschweiler, *Neujahrsblatt der Zurcher Kunstgesellschaft*, 1966/67, pp. 96–97, fig. 99–101.
A poster design for the Künstlerhaus in Zurich, this work was never printed, though the drawing was exhibited at the Vienna Secession in 1904. In this composition, Hodler renders line in a characteristic Art Nouveau idiom. The prostrate male figure presages his later large composition, *Love*.

81. *The Dream*. (1897). Graphite under gouache and pen and ink on brown wove paper. 38⅝ x 27⅛". Collection Mrs. M. Meyer, Zurich.
Signed, lower right, in pen and ink: F. Hodler.
Unpublished.
Like no. 80, "The Dream" is a compositional

design for a poster. It too employs a Jugendstil line, a flat, curvilinear line that renders form into pattern and shape into a network of repeated planes hovering close to the surface of the picture. According to Mr. Brüschweiler this poster design was also meant for the Künstlerhaus in Zurich and exhibited at the Vienna Secession in 1904 (Secession cat. no. 30).

*82. *Compositional Study for "Day I."* (ca. 1897). Graphite under watercolor, pen and ink, on brown wove paper. 6⅞ x 20½". Kunstmuseum Bern. [Ill. p. 89.]
Signed in graphite at lower right: F. Hodler.
Reference: Jura Brüschweiler, *Ferdinand Hodler Dessins*, Musée Rath, 1963, no. 107.
See discussion in catalogue essay on Hodler's draftsmanship.

*83. *Compositional Study for "Day I."* (ca. 1898). Graphite under watercolor (pastel and water) on cream laid paper. 7⅝ x 18⅞". Kunsthaus Zurich (Z Inv. 1919/36). [Ill. p. 89.]
Signed, lower right: F.H.
Reference: Jura Brüschweiler, *Ferdinand Hodler Dessins*, Musée Rath, 1963, no. 111.
See discussion in catalogue essay on Hodler's draftsmanship.

84. *Figure Study for "Day I."* (ca. 1898). Graphite on cream wove paper, lightly squared (before figure drawn). 4¾ x 4". Kunsthaus Zurich (Hodler Archives no. 1009z).
Signed in graphite, lower right: F. Hodler.
Unpublished.
See discussion in catalogue essay on Hodler's draftsmanship.

85. *Studies for Figure in "Day I."* (ca. 1898). Graphite on white Fabriano paper, lightly squared beforehand. 5⅞ x 19⅛". Collection Kurt Meissner, Zurich (M-15).
Stamped twice in lower right: Ferd. Hodler, in ink, and dry estate stamp above.
Reference: Jura Brüschweiler, catalogue of Hodler drawings from the Meissner Collection, Zurich, in preparation.
See discussion in catalogue essay on Hodler's draftsmanship.

*86. *Figure Study for "Day I."* (ca. 1898–1899). Graphite on white wove paper, squared beforehand. 8½ x 6⅝". Collection Kurt Meissner, Zurich (M-23). [Ill. p. 89.]
Stamped twice in lower right: Ferd. Hodler, in ink, and dry estate stamp above.
Reference: Jura Brüschweiler, catalogue of Hodler drawings from the Meissner Collection, Zurich, in preparation.
See discussion in catalogue essay on Hodler's draftsmanship.

87. *Compositional Study for "Day I."* (ca. 1899). Graphite under china ink and wash, heightened with watercolor and gouache, on cream wove paper. Partial collage. 8¾ x 4⅜". Kunsthaus Zurich (Z Inv. 1919/37).
Signed lower right in brush and ink: F. Hodler.

Reference: Jura Brüschweiler, *Ferdinand Hodler Dessins*, Musée Rath, 1963, no. 117.
See discussion in catalogue essay on Hodler's draftsmanship.

88. *Figure Study for "Emotion."* (1901–1902). Graphite under watercolor and pastel on paper; collage figure on paper mount. 12⅜ x 5⅛". Collection Josef Müller, Solothurn.
Unsigned.
Unpublished.
Given by the artist to his supporter and most distinguished collector, Mr. Josef Müller, this unpublished drawing, in collage, traces the flowing contours of a form in implied motion, with drapery energized by the figure's movement.

89. *Study for "Truth II."* (ca. 1902). Graphite under china ink and watercolor, on white paper, squared beforehand. 13¾ x 19⅞". Private Collection, Geneva.
Signed at lower right: Ferd. Hodler.
Reference: Jura Brüschweiler, *Ferdinand Hodler Dessins*, Musée Rath, 1963, no. 142.
This compositional study for the painting entitled *Truth II* (no. 25), of 1902 (Kunsthaus Zurich) reuses a figure motif from *Day* and the poster design, *Poetry* (no. 80). The central figure, now standing, is posed with her arms bent and spread out in a lateral direction, parallel in the plane to her head. The receding draped, male forms recall those in *Eurythmy*, of 1895 (Kunstmuseum Bern). The study, as opposed to the two painted versions, delineates the figural forms with contours not yet regularized, as if still in search of their final, determining shapes.

90. *Figure Study for "The Departure of the Volunteers in 1813."* (1907–1908). Graphite on white paper. 14¼ x 5⅜". Friedrich Schiller University, Jena.
Unsigned. Authenticated on verso by Mme. Berthe Hodler.
Reference: *Fall Hodler: Jena 1914–1919*, Friedrich-Schiller-Universität, 1970, pl. a.
This figure study, as well as nos. 91 and 92, is rendered with an open contour line that delineates the form of the marching figure with a minimal amount of interior details. The artist is searching for the most satisfying position of the soldier's left arm. Hodler's abbreviated drawing style reveals the artist's skill in drawing a fully mobile, aesthetically pleasing and decorative figural form.

91. *Figure Study for "The Departure of the Volunteers in 1813."* (1907–1908). Graphite on white paper. 11½ x 16¼". Friedrich Schiller University, Jena.
Unsigned. Authenticated on verso by Mme. Berthe Hodler.
Reference: *Fall Hodler: Jena 1914–1919*, Friedrich-Schiller-Universität, 1970, pl. c.
See entry no. 90.

*92. *Figure Study for "The Departure of the Volunteers in 1813."* (1907–1908). Recto: graphite on Fabriano paper. Verso: black, red oil paint. 22½ x 17½". Kunsthaus Zurich (Hodler Archives no. 1009y). [Ill. p. 79.]
Estate stamp, in lower right.
Unpublished.
See discussion in catalogue essay on Hodler's draftsmanship.

93. *Figure Group for "The Departure of the Volunteers in 1813."* (1907–1908). Graphite under black ink painted with brush, on Fabriano paper. 17⅜ x 8¼". Oeffentliche Kunstsammlung Basel (Kupferstichkabinett).
Signed in graphite and inscribed, lower right: F. Hodler fur Jena.
Unpublished.
This figure group, a study for the painted mural of the same subject, combines the open-contour line of nos. 90–92 with an ink wash treatment that creates an interplay of line and shape, positive and negative areas of black and white masses. The implied brevity of execution and the combination of pictorial elements recall Manet's draftsmanship.

94. *Compositional Study for "The Departure of the Volunteers in 1813."* (1908). Graphite with stumping on tan paper. 24⅜ x 36⅞". Musée d'Art et d'Histoire, Geneva (Inv. no. 1939.114).
Signed at lower right: F. Hodler.
Reference: Jura Brüschweiler, *Ferdinand Hodler Dessins*, Musée Rath, 1963, no. 162.
A full compositional study in graphite, drawn and stumped in a range of tones, this work closely approximates the final painting at the Friedrich Schiller University in Jena. The drawing is so complete and meticulous in the rendering of detail that it was probably intended to represent the final version of the painting, executed before or even after the commissioned work.

95. *Compositional Study for "Love."* (1904–1907). Graphite on cream-colored paper. 15 x 18⅛". Collection Josef Müller, Solothurn.
Signed in graphite with monogram, lower right: F H.
Unpublished.
See discussion in catalogue essay on Hodler's draftsmanship.

*96. *Study for "Love."* (1908). Graphite on white wove paper. 9⅛ x 14½". Collection Bruno Giacometti, Zurich. [Ill. p. 75.]
Signed lower right: F. Hodler.
Unpublished.
See discussion in catalogue essay on Hodler's draftsmanship.

*97. *Study for "Love."* (1907–1908). Graphite on tracing paper, squared. 8½ x 14⅝". Collection Kurt Meissner, Zurich (M-94). [Ill. p. 77.]
Stamped twice, in lower right corner: Ferd. Hodler (purple ink stamp) and dry estate stamp above.

Reference: Jura Brüschweiler, catalogue of
Hodler drawings from the Meissner Collection, Zurich, in preparation.
See discussion in catalogue essay on Hodler's
draftsmanship.

*98. *Lovers.* (1907–1908). Soft graphite on tracing
paper, squared before drawing. 5⅛ x 10¼".
University Art Museum, Berkeley. [Ill. p. 77.]
Stamped: authenticated on verso by Mme.
Berthe Hodler.
Unpublished.
See discussion in catalogue essay on Hodler's
draftsmanship.

99. *Figure Studies for "The Sacred Hour" (II bis).*
(ca. 1908). Graphite on tracing paper.
21⅝ x 17⅛". Collection Kurt Meissner,
Zurich (M-73).
Stamped with two stamps in lower corners:
right, Ferd. Hodler (purple ink), and dry
estate stamp, at left.
Reference: Jura Brüschweiler, catalogue of
Hodler drawings from the Meissner Collection, Zurich, in preparation.
On this sheet of six studies of the same
figure, Hodler illustrates his pictorial thought
process, how he moves in almost minute
steps to change the drapery of this figure
until its lines effect the proper pattern that
satisfies the artist's objectives.

*100. *Valentine Godé-Darel Wearing a Hat.*
(1909). Graphite on notebook sheet paper,
printed as graph paper. 6¼ x 4". Collection
Kurt Meissner, Zurich. [Ill. p. 91.]
Stamped lower right, in purple ink: Ferd.
Hodler. Estate stamp lower left(?). Inscribed
lower left: Mme. Godé Darel (not in the
artist's hand).
Reference: Jura Brüschweiler, catalogue of
Hodler drawings from the Meissner Collection, Zurich, in preparation.
See discussion in catalogue essay on Hodler's
draftsmanship.

*101. *Valentine Godé-Darel in Silhouette.*
(ca. 1909). Graphite on white Fabriano
paper. 18⅞ x 13¼". Collection Rudolf-
Emil Schindler, Ligerz. [Ill. p. 93.]
Stamped with dry estate stamp
lower right.
Unpublished.
See discussion in catalogue essay on
Hodler's draftsmanship.

*102. *Figure Study for "Woman with Arms
Spread Apart."* (1908/1909). Graphite on
white Fabriano paper, with monotype in
oil on verso. 14⅛ x 10". Collection Kurt
Meissner, Zurich (M-153). [Ill. p. 93.]
Signed in graphite at lower right: F.
Hodler.
Reference: Jura Brüschweiler, catalogue
of Hodler drawings from the Meissner
Collection, Zurich, in preparation.
See discussion in catalogue essay on
Hodler's draftsmanship.

103. *Giulia Leonardi and her Sister-in-Law.*
(1910). Graphite on white Fabriano paper
(an uncut sheet). 17¼ x 23". Collection
Kurt Meissner, Zurich (M-257).
Stamped with two stamps, lower left:
Ferd. Hodler (purple ink), and dry
estate stamp.
Reference: Jura Brüschweiler, catalogue
of Hodler drawings from the Meissner
Collection, Zurich, in preparation.
Drawn in the abbreviated open-contour
style of nos. 90, 91, and 101, this double
portrait was no doubt inspired by an
evening at the cabaret in which Giulia
performed. The two forms sway to the
music of her guitar. The exaggerated
scale and seemingly awkward foreshortening of Giulia's left foot, in the foreground of the composition, realistically
depict her actual club foot.

*104. *The Great Joys of Life (Floraison).* (ca.
1911–1913). Collage of figures cut out
of cream wove paper, drawing in graph-
ite, appliqued to brown paper, with ink
and gouache. 29½ x 39⅜". Collection
Rudolf-Emil Schindler, Ligerz. [Ill. p. 83.]
Signed: estate stamp, lower right.
Unpublished.
See discussion in catalogue essay on
Hodler's draftsmanship.

105. *Three Female Figures (Study for a
decoration at the Kunsthaus Zurich).*
(ca. 1911–1913). Graphite on white
Fabriano paper. 12¾ x 17¼". Collection
Kurt Meissner, Zurich (M-166).
Stamped with two stamps in lower
corners: Ferd. Hodler in purple ink,
lower left, and dry estate stamp
at lower right.
Reference: Jura Brüschweiler, catalogue
of Hodler drawings from the Meissner
Collection, Zurich, in preparation.
Reduced to their essential contours,
these three female forms create a set
of arabesque lines, gracefully forming a
network of repeated arcs and shapes, of
figure and ground. Hodler's theory of
Parallelism is here defined graphically.

*106. *Valentine Godé-Darel (Profile to Right).*
(1913). Graphite on cream wove paper.
12¼ x 9¼". Collection Rudolf-Emil
Schindler, Ligerz. [Ill. p. 95.]
Unsigned. Authenticated on verso by
Mme. Berthe Hodler.
Unpublished.
See discussion in catalogue essay on
Hodler's draftsmanship.

*107. *Valentine Godé-Darel, Ill.* (1914). Graph-
ite with stumping on tan wove paper.
Monotype drawing in red oil on verso.
18½ x 20⅛". Musée d'Art et d'Histoire,
Geneva (Inv. no. 1964. 69). [Ill. p. 95.]
Signed in graphite at lower right: F.
Hodler. Inscribed below signature:

p. a v (pas à vendre).
Reference: Jura Brüschweiler, *Catalogue des oeuvres de Ferdinand Hodler léguées au Musée d'Art et d'Histoire par M. et Mme. Hector Hodler-Ruch: Extrait de Genève, XIII, 1965*, Geneva, 1965, p. 189.
See discussion in catalogue essay on Hodler's draftsmanship.

*108. *Valentine and Pauline.* 1914. Graphite on yellowed Japan paper. 12¼ x 18½". Kunstmuseum Bern (Bequest of Mme. Hector Hodler, 1964). [Ill. p. 97.]
Signed and dated (to left of signature) in graphite, lower right: Ferd. Hodler. 1914.
Unpublished.
See discussion in catalogue essay on Hodler's draftsmanship.

*109. *Valentine Godé-Darel, in Bed.* 1914. Graphite on cream-colored paper. 18½ x 24½". Musée d'Art et d'Histoire, Geneva. [Ill. p. 97.]
Signed, dated, and inscribed at the lower right: Titine / p. a v / 8 Nov. / Ferd Hodler.
Reference: Jura Brüschweiler, *Ferdinand Hodler Dessins*, Musée Rath, 1963, no. 199.
See discussion in catalogue essay on Hodler's draftsmanship.

*110. *Valentine Godé-Darel, Asleep.* 1915. Graphite on cream wove paper. 18½ x 12¼". Kunsthaus Zurich (Z Inv. 1917/31). [Ill. p. 99.]
Signed, dated, inscribed in graphite, lower right: 1915 / F. Hodler / p. a v.
Reference: Jura Brüschweiler, *Ferdinand Hodler Dessins*, Musée Rath, 1963, no. 204.
See discussion in catalogue essay on Hodler's draftsmanship.

*111. *Valentine Godé-Darel, Asleep.* 1915. Graphite heightened with white gouache, on gray Fabriano paper. 13¼ x 19⅛". Kunstmuseum Bern (Inv. A7684). [Ill. p. 99.]
Signed, dated, and inscribed, in graphite, lower right: 1915 / F Hodler / An Hans Muhlestein / F.H.
Reference: Jura Brüschweiler, *Ferdinand Hodler Dessins*, Musée Rath, 1963, no. 205.
See discussion in catalogue essay on Hodler's draftsmanship.

112. *Valentine Godé-Darel, in Agony.* 1915. Graphite on cream wove paper. Monotype image in black oil on verso. 18½ x 24½". Kunsthaus Zurich (Z Inv. 1964/19).
Signed, dated, and inscribed in graphite, at lower right: 1915 / 19 Janv. / F.H. / p. a v.
Reference: Jura Brüschweiler, *Neujahrsblatt der Zurcher Kunstgesellschaft*, 1966/1967, p. 111.

See discussion in catalogue essay on Hodler's draftsmanship.

*113. *Valentine Godé-Darel, near Death.* 1915. Graphite under gouache on beige paper. 13½ x 17⅞". Kunsthaus Zurich (Z Inv. 1917/32). [Ill. p. 101.]
Signed and inscribed with the date, by the artist, in the lower right corner: 1915 / 24 Janv / F Hodler.
Reference: Jura Brüschweiler, *Ferdinand Hodler Dessins*, Musée Rath, 1963, no. 207.
See discussion in catalogue essay on Hodler's draftsmanship.

*114. *Valentine Godé-Darel, Dead.* 1915. Oil on paper. 15½ x 25¼". Oeffentliche Kunstsammlung Basel (Kupferstichkabinett). [Ill. p. 101.]
Signed and dated, in oil, at lower right: F. Hodler / 26 Janv / 1915.
Reference: Kunstmuseum Basel catalogue 19/20, 1970, p. 64.
See discussion in catalogue essay on Hodler's draftsmanship.

*115. *Self-portrait.* 1915. Charcoal with white oil paint, on tracing paper mounted on cardboard. 15⅝ x 12¾". Musée d'Art et d'Histoire, Geneva (Inv. no. 1939.80). [Ill. p. 103.]
Signed, dated, and inscribed, in graphite, at lower right: Neris / 1915 / F. Hodler.
Reference: Jura Brüschweiler, *Ferdinand Hodler Dessins*, Musée Rath, 1963, no. 210.
See discussion in catalogue essay on Hodler's draftsmanship.

116. *Three Preliminary Sketches for "The Battle of Morat."* (ca. 1915). Pen and black ink on cream wove paper. Kunsthaus Zurich.
a. 5¼ x 8¼" (Hodler Archives no. 562).
b. 5⅛ x 8⅜" (Hodler Archives no. 564).
c. 4⅞ x 8⅜" (Hodler Archives no. 561).
Unsigned.
Unpublished.
These small sketches should be read as "ideas" for the eventual painted wall-scale composition of 1917, today located at the Musée d'Art et d'Histoire, Geneva, and the Schweizerisches Landesmuseum, Zurich. They reveal Hodler's thought process as he draws out a pictorial concept, here a battle with lunging human figures and repeating linear shapes that eventually form the compositional lines of force.

117. *Six Preliminary Sketches for "Floraison"* (1916–1918). Pen and ink, sometimes over graphite underdrawing, on red or blue squared printed graph paper.
*a. 3¼ x 8⅛". Kunsthaus Zurich (Hodler Archives no. 511). [Ill. p. 81.]
*b. 4¾ x 7⅞". Mounted as verso of c.

Kunsthaus Zurich (Hodler Archives no. 11.) [Ill. p. 81.]

   c. 4¾ x 7⅞''. Mounted as verso. Kunsthaus Zurich (Hodler Archives no. 12).

*d. 4⅝ x 7⅞''. Kunsthaus Zurich (Hodler Archives no. 517). [Ill. p. 81.]

*e. 4⅞ x 8¼''. Kunsthaus Zurich (Hodler Archives no. 513). [Ill. p. 81.]

   f. 5¼ x 8⅜''. Kunsthaus Zurich (Hodler Archives no. 512).

   g. 5¼ x 8⅛''. Private Collection, Geneva.

Unpublished.

See discussion in catalogue essay on Hodler's draftsmanship.

118. *Four Preliminary Sketches for Mountain Landscapes.* (1915–1918). Pen and black ink on red squared graph paper, or graphite on cream-colored wove paper.

   a. 7½ x 10⅜''. Kunsthaus Zurich (Hodler Archives no. 276).

   b. 7½ x 10½''. Kunsthaus Zurich (Hodler Archives no. 278).

   c. 8¾ x 12⅝''. Kunsthaus Zurich (Hodler Archives no. 271). Reference: C. A. Loosli, *Ferdinand Hodler: Leben, Werk und Nachlass*, vol. II, pl. 26.

   d. "The Voirons, the Môle, the chain of Mont-Blanc, and the little Salève." 1918. Graphite. 4⅜ x 8⅜''. Private Collection, Geneva.

Unsigned.

Reference: Jura Brüschweiler, *Ferdinand Hodler Dessins*, Musée Rath, 1963, no. 248.

These sketches enable us once again to see Hodler's thought process, already graphed in nos. 116 and 117, now applied to a landscape composition. With an economy of line, either in pen and ink or graphite, Hodler blocks out a scene, sometimes enframed as he might have seen it from his studio window (118-c). His scene is always constructed on a horizontal format, in which lateral planes line up vertically rather than moving back into an illusionistic space. The foreground "space" is left empty, flat, as if to open the viewer's eyes to the grandeur of the mountain forms that remain eternally present.

Ferdinand Hodler in his studio on the Rue du Rhone in Geneva, before "Emotion" and "Day II" (ca. 1906). [Photo courtesy Jura Brüschweiler, Geneva, ©].

Lenders to the Exhibition

Jura Brüschweiler, Geneva
B. Gerald Cantor, Beverly Hills
Mrs. Gertrud Dübi, Solothurn
Dr. A. Gerber, Zurich
Bruno Giacometti, Zurich
Professor Hans R. Hahnloser, Bern
J. J. Kurz, Zurich
Messrs. Maus & Nordmann, Geneva
Kurt Meissner, Zurich
Mrs. M. Meyer, Zurich
Josef Müller, Solothurn
Rudolf-Emil Schindler, Ligerz
Dr. h. c. Max Schmidheiny, Heerbrugg
Claude Schmidt, Geneva
Mr. and Mrs. Robert M. Schwarzenbach,
  Norwalk, Connecticut

Oeffentliche Kunstsammlung Basel
University Art Museum, Berkeley
Kunstmuseum Bern
The Detroit Institute of Arts
Musée d'Art et d'Histoire, Geneva
Kunstmuseum Lucerne
Musée d'Art et d'Histoire, Neuchatel
Kunstmuseum Olten
Kunstmuseum St. Gallen
Museum zu Allerheiligen Schaffhausen
Friedrich Schiller University, Jena, German
  Democratic Republic
Museum der Stadt Solothurn
Kunstmuseum Winterthur
Kunsthaus Zurich
Kunstgewerbemuseum Zurich

Contributors

This exhibition and accompanying catalogue
were made possible by the active and financial
support of Pro Helvetia Foundation, and by the
financial support of the following contributors:

Corporations:

C. F. Bally Ltd., Zurich
Bank Rüd Blass, Zurich
Bank Leu AG, Zurich
Bank Populaire Suisse, Bern
Bank Ruegg & Co. AG, Zurich
Julius Bär & Co., Zurich
Brown Boveri Corporation, North Brunswick,
  New Jersey
Ciba-Geigy Corporation, Ardsley, New York
Ebauches S.A., Neuchatel
Eterna Watch Co., Grenchen
George Fischer Ltd., Schaffhausen
Gübelin Ltd., Lucerne
Helsa H. Saner AG, Studen bei Brügg
Heuer-Leonidas SA, Biel-Bienne
Hoffmann-La Roche, Inc., Nutley, New Jersey
Cement Works Holderbank-Wildegg, Holderbank

IBM Schweiz, Zurich
S. Kocher & Co. SA, Eska & Royce Watches,
  Grenchen
Kraftwerk Laufenburg
Lindt & Sprüngli Ltd., Kilchberg
Loeb Frères S.A., Bern
Federation of Migros Co-operatives, Zurich
Nestlé Company, White Plains, New York
Nivada Watch Co. Ltd., Grenchen
Philip Morris Switzerland, Neuchatel
Montres Rolex S.A., Geneva
A. Sarasin & Cie., Basel
Schweizerische Mobiliar, Bern
Chocolat Suchard SA, Neuchatel
Sulzer Bros. Inc., New York
Swiss Bank Corporation, Basel
Swiss Center, New York
Swiss Credit Bank, Zurich
Swiss Reinsurance Co., Zurich
Union Bank of Switzerland, Zurich
Waltham Watch Company, Chicago
Accident and Casualty Insurance Company,
  Winterthur

Cantons/Cities/Foundations/Private:

Canton of Basel-Stadt
Canton of Bern
Canton of Fribourg
Canton of Geneva
Canton of Solothurn
Canton of Zurich

City of Bern
City of Zurich

Alcoa Foundation, Pittsburgh, Pennsylvania
Burlington Industries Foundation,
  Greensboro, North Carolina
Ulrico Hoepli Foundation, Zurich
Pro Helvetia Foundation, Zurich
Sandoz Foundation, New York
The Swiss Society of New York
Marguerite and Alfred Wyler Foundation,
  New York

Mrs. Rudolf P. Bircher, New York
Mr. William W. Heer, New York
Dr. Anton K. Maier, Madison, New Jersey
Mr. Kurt Meissner, Zurich
Mrs. Mary B. Rohner, New York
Mr. Albert Ruth, New York
Dr. h. c. Max Schmidheiny, Heerbrugg

Photography Credits

Most photographs were provided by respective
lenders without specified credit; those specified
photographers are as follows:

Walter Dräyer, Zurich, pp. 75 and 101
Phyllis Hattis, San Francisco, pp. 85, 75, 93, 83, 95, and 81
Colin McRae, Berkeley, pp. 72, 77, and 103
Photo Routhier, Paris, p. 73
Jean Zbinden, Geneva, pp. 69, 65, 47 (bottom), 39
(top), and cover

10,000 copies of this catalogue designed by
Bruce Montgomery, San Francisco, have been
printed in November 1972 on the occasion of
the exhibition *Ferdinand Hodler*. Typography
is Trump regular and bold, set by Spartan
Typographers, Oakland. Offset lithography is by
California Printing Company, San Francisco.
Black and white reproductions are printed in
200 line screen single and double blacks, four
color reproductions are in 150 line screen and
spot varnished. Cover paper is 12 point
Kromekote. Text paper is 80 lb. Cameo Brilliant,
dull finish.